DISCOVERING U.S. HISTORY

Colonial America

1543–1763

DISCOVERING U.S. HISTORY

The New World: Prehistory–1542

Colonial America: 1543–1763

Revolutionary America: 1764–1789

Early National America: 1790–1850

The Civil War Era: 1851–1865

The New South and the Old West: 1866–1890

The Gilded Age and Progressivism: 1891–1913

World War I and the Roaring Twenties: 1914–1928

The Great Depression: 1929–1938

World War II: 1939–1945

The Cold War and Postwar America: 1946–1963

Modern America: 1964–Present

DISCOVERING U.S. HISTORY

Colonial America
1543–1763

Tim McNeese

Consulting Editor: Richard Jensen, Ph.D.

CHELSEA HOUSE
PUBLISHERS
An imprint of Infobase Publishing

COLONIAL AMERICA 1543–1763

Copyright © 2010 by Infobase Publishing

Chelsea House
An imprint of Infobase Publishing
132 West 31st Street
New York NY 10001

Library of Congress Cataloging-in-Publication Data
McNeese, Tim.
   Colonial America, 1543-1763 / by Tim McNeese.
      p. cm. — (Discovering U.S. history)
   Includes bibliographical references and index.
   ISBN 978-1-60413-349-3 (hardcover : acid-free paper) 1. United States—History—Colonial period,
   ca. 1600-1775—Juvenile literature. 2. United States—History—Revolution, 1775-1783—Juvenile
   literature. I. Title. II. Series.

E188.M18 2009
973.2—dc22

                              2008055170

Chelsea House books are available at special discounts when purchased in
bulk quantities for businesses, associations, institutions, or sales promotions.
Please call our Special Sales Department in New York at (212) 967-8800
or (800) 322-8755.

You can find Chelsea House on the World Wide Web at http://www.chelseahouse.com

The Discovering U.S. History series was produced for Chelsea House
by Bender Richardson White, Uxbridge, UK

Editors: Lionel Bender and Clare Hibbert
Designer: Ben White
Production: Kim Richardson
Maps and graphics: Stefan Chabluk
Picture Research: Susannah Jayes
Cover printed by Bang Printing, Brainerd, MN
Book printed and bound by Bang Printing, Brainerd, MN
Date printed: April 2010
Printed in the United States of America

10 9 8 7 6 5 4 3 2 1

This book is printed on acid-free paper.

All links and web addresses were checked and verified to be correct at the time of publication. Because of
the dynamic nature of the web, some addresses and links may have changed since publication and may no
longer be valid.

Contents

Introduction
The Pilgrims Set Sail

For too many years the congregation of Separatists that worshiped in the country village of Scrooby in Nottinghamshire, England, struggled to maintain its fellowship. The time was the early 1600s, and history remembers these oppressed worshipers as the Pilgrims. Part of a conscience-driven Protestant sect, these Reformation-era Englishmen and women had been constantly persecuted by the Crown, their religious services interrupted, their leaders punished, and their future always in doubt. The government oppressed such groups because they challenged the authority of the Church of England. The king, James I, declared that the Separatists must follow the forms of worship of the Church of England or he would "harry [chase] them out of the land."

Times had become so uncertain for the Separatists that they fled England to Leiden, Holland, but they felt the culture there was too liberal and feared its influence upon their children.

THE PROMISE OF NEW ENGLAND

The solution to the group's dilemma emerged from an unlikely place and person. Puritan leaders William Brewster and William Bradford both read Captain John Smith's 1616 book, *A Description of New England*, which chronicled his establishment in the spring of 1607 of Jamestown, the first successful English colony in North America. Brewster and

The *Mayflower* was a sturdy sailing vessel about 90 feet (27 meters) long and 25 feet (7.6 m) wide. It was a merchant ship with a crew of about 30 men.

Bradford began making plans for their followers to try practicing their faith in a new location—America.

By September 1620 a party of 102 men, women, and children were ready to leave. After two delayed starts, the Pilgrims sailed from Southampton, England, across the Atlantic on the crowded *Mayflower*. Conditions on board the ship were miserable. The vessel was in poor condition, the water onboard soured, food molded due to the ocean dampness, and flour barrels were soon crawling with maggots and weevils. In addition, high winds and a damaged ship created dangerous conditions.

On November 9 the nightmare ended as the *Mayflower* finally came within sight of land. Although the Pilgrims had set sail for Virginia, the storms had blown them off course to the north. The ship's crewmembers scanned the horizon and decided they were offshore from the highlands of Cape Cod, in the New England that John Smith had written about in his book. The great arm of the cape provided a natural barrier and harbor, and a welcome calm after the storms that had battered the *Mayflower*.

PURITAN COLONY

The colonists decided to remain in this location and build their colony, a New World outpost that promised new opportunity, including the freedom to worship as they pleased.

Yet so many questions lay ahead. What was the land before them like? Would it support their number? Had storms flung them here because it was God's choice for them? Would life be better here? What was God's plan for his people?

History records the arrival of the Pilgrims on the shores of lands that would one day be known as Massachusetts. It does not record how many American Indians were already on those shores, observing the Pilgrims and their great canoe that floated in the water, its sails billowing like clouds.

Colonial America

Starting with the Jamestown settlement in Virginia in 1607, English, French, Spanish, and Dutch settlers set up colonies along the eastern seaboard of North America. From these territories, Europeans spread west and by 1750 they had claimed most of the east and southwest of present-day USA.

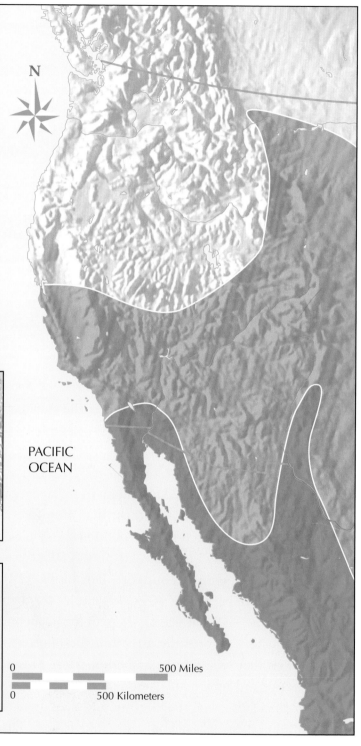

PACIFIC
OCEAN

0   500 Miles

0   500 Kilometers

ALASKA

N

0   500 Miles

0   500 Kilometers

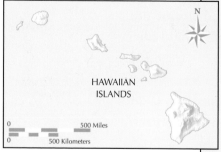

HAWAIIAN
ISLANDS

0   500 Miles

0   500 Kilometers

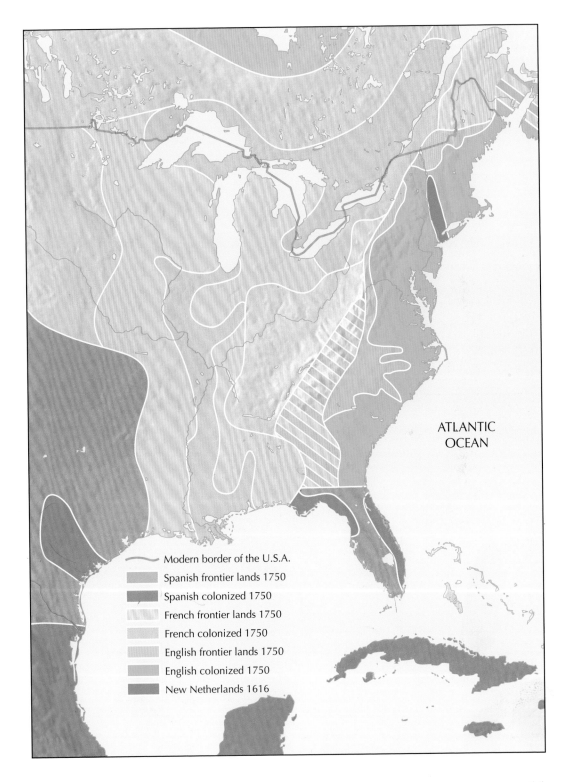

ATLANTIC
OCEAN

Modern border of the U.S.A.

Spanish frontier lands 1750

Spanish colonized 1750

French frontier lands 1750

French colonized 1750

English frontier lands 1750

English colonized 1750

New Netherlands 1616

1 Rivals for North America

Perhaps no other event in European history had a greater impact on U.S. history than Christopher Columbus's 1492 voyage of discovery. Searching for a short, westerly route to the spices and wealth of Asia, Columbus had sailed across the Atlantic only to reach new lands that would become known as North, Central, and South America. The Genoan sea captain and mapmaker died in 1506 poor and nearly forgotten, but his dream of reaching China and the Spice Islands had opened up whole continents—regardless of whether the indigenous populations would welcome further European exploration and settlement.

SPANISH POWER

Columbus had sailed under the sponsorship of the Spanish monarchy. During the decades that followed, Spain became the first European power to establish an extensive system of colonies. Through representatives of the Spanish king—

including priests, merchants, landowners, and soldiers or conquistadores—Spain staked its claims to the lands, wealth, and even the native peoples of the Americas. As Spain colonized, it focused most of its efforts on lands that were south of the modern-day United States.

Spain was the first to take advantage of its opportunities in the New World, but other European leaders were soon eyeing Spain's successes with jealousy. They mounted sea voyages of their own, targeting lands north of most of Spain's early outposts.

ENGLAND SENDS JOHN CABOT

England was one of the first rivals to Spain in the New World. Just five years after Columbus reached the Caribbean, the English Crown sponsored another Genoan, John Cabot, to sail on its behalf. Little is known of Cabot, not even when he was born or the exact year of his death. Even his name is in question: alternatives include Giovanni or Zuan Caboto. It is known that Cabot was a merchant in Venice during the 1460s and that by 1490 he had moved with his three sons—Ludovico, Sancto, and Sebastian—to England, where he became a respected merchant and sea captain.

While living in England, Cabot developed a theory similar to that of Columbus—that the Orient could be easiest reached by sailing west across the Atlantic. Cabot's vision differed from Columbus's, however. He thought Japan lay directly west of England, placing it north of the Caribbean. Cabot became convinced that Columbus had landed too far south of the Spice Islands when he reached America in 1492. He set out to find a sponsor, much as Columbus had done a decade earlier, to provide support for his theory. Cabot received such backing from England's King Henry VII. In the spring of 1496 Henry gave Cabot permission to sail west to Asia with royal funding for his ships and supplies.

Cabot's voyage proved a difficult one. Lackluster winds and a supply shortage caused him to return to England before reaching his goal. The following year he set sail again onboard the *Matthew* with a crew of 18, plus his son, Sebastian. After more than seven weeks at sea, the ship made landfall on June 24, 1497, at a place Cabot called "new found land" (probably Canada's Labrador, Newfoundland, or Cape Breton Island). Five centuries had passed since Viking longships had arrived along those same shores. After several weeks of exploring, Cabot returned to England, where an enthusiastic King Henry gave him the title of Great Admiral and authorized another voyage for the following year. Cabot was now so famous that, according to historian Peter Hoffer, everywhere he went on the streets of London, "the English ran after him like mad people."

CABOT'S FINAL VOYAGE

For his 1498 voyage, Cabot's single ship became five and his crew numbered 300 men. But, once again, troubles plagued the Genoan sea captain. A storm hit the English flotilla and damaged one of the ships, forcing its early return to England while Cabot and his other four ships continued on to America. In the event, the returning vessel became the voyage's sole survivor, for Cabot and his other ships never came back and the mystery of their disappearance remains today.

Nevertheless, Henry VII still based his claim to the lands of North America on Cabot's voyages of discovery. That claim was furthered by Cabot's son, Sebastian, who commanded voyages to the New World in 1508 and 1526. During his time in America, Sebastian reached Hudson Bay, giving England an additional claim to the North American interior. Other voyages from England involved merchants, both English and Portuguese, whom Henry VII sent to Newfoundland to establish trade with the American Indians. Little came of any of these efforts in the short run. The king refused to invest any significant money in the New World, a position later held by his son, Henry VIII, and his grandchildren, Edward VI and Mary I.

VERRAZANO AND THE NORTHWEST PASSAGE

The French entered the exploring business and the competition for New World riches several years later. In 1523 King Francis I dispatched yet another Italian seafarer, Giovanni da Verrazano, to the New World to make claims in the monarch's name. The king also charged Verrazano to search for the fabled Northwest Passage, an assumed all-water route around the northern reaches of North America that would deliver a ship to the other side of the Western Hemisphere and on to the spices and wealth of Asia. (Yet no such ice-free corridor existed then or now, even though others continued the search for the passage into the nineteenth century.)

As Cabot had trouble with storms in the North Atlantic, so did Verrazano, whose fleet of four ships was reduced to a single vessel during his 1524 voyage. In April that ship, the *Dauphin,* arrived off the coast of Newfoundland, which Cabot had already claimed for England. Proceeding south, Verrazano sailed all the way to modern-day South Carolina. He reached today's New York Harbor where he traded with some local Indians, who impressed him with their hospitality. He was also impressed in his dealings with the Wampanoag Indians of today's New England. (A century later, the Pilgrims on the *Mayflower* also reached the lands of the Wampanoags.)

Verrazano did not like his encounters with the Abenaki in modern-day Maine, however, whom he described, as noted by historian Peter Charles Hoffer, as savages after he "found no courtesy in them, and when we had nothing more to exchange and left them, the men made all the signs of scorn and shame that any brute creature would make."

The American Indians not only traded with the new arrivals from Europe, they also provided information. Verrazano heard stories of a large Indian city off to the north, which they called "Norumbega." They also informed him that this city was located at the entrance to the Northwest Passage.

European explorers were looking for riches. This colored woodcut from Italian Girolamo Benzoni's *La Historia del Mondo Nuovo* of 1565 shows American Indians melting and working gold and silver.

Without finding it, the Venetian sea captain returned to France and informed the king of his discoveries. But even a claim of the existence of the Northwest Passage was not enough for Francis I to send Verrazano back to America. He had fallen into war with Spain and was prepared to rival the Spanish on the battlefield, not on the fields of the New World. Verrazano's voyage to North America became a dead end to French colonization in the western hemisphere.

CARTIER SAILS FOR FRANCE

By 1532 King Francis had concluded his war with Spain and established a fragile peace. The French king soon gave audience to another would-be explorer, a fellow Frenchman named Jacques Cartier. He told Francis his intention to find the Northwest Passage, referring back to Verrazano's claims. Francis could not have chosen more wisely than Cartier. In

FRENCH FISHING SETTLEMENTS

In contrast with the king, others in France were not so easily distracted from Verrazano's successes. By the 1530s French fishermen from Brittany and Normandy gathered small fleets of boats and headed across the Atlantic to cast their nets in the New World. In the same waters crisscrossed by Cabot and Verrazano, they established fishing villages, where they brought in huge catches of cod and other prized sea fish from the fishing banks off Nova Scotia and Newfoundland. With millions of cod available, the Europeans placed their catches wet and salted in barrels. They would fish until they had filled a boat with barrels, then sail back to France, dump their lucrative cargo, and return for a second round of fishing before the season ended. While the settlements they established only operated seasonally, these fishermen and sea captains represented at least some French presence in the New World.

1534 the seaman was 43 years old, a talented navigator and sea captain, and a veteran of sailing the Atlantic. The historian Thomas Costain described him as "a stocky man with a sharply etched profile and calm eyes under a high, wide brow . . . and with a beard which bristled pugnaciously." Between 1534 and 1542 Cartier sailed to North America three times, exploring the region of Newfoundland and Labrador.

Cartier's voyages to the New World are considered models of successful exploration because he never lost a single ship or crewmember. On his first voyage in 1534, he reached Newfoundland from France with two ships in just three weeks' of sailing. After a few more weeks of exploring, he arrived at the Gulf of St. Lawrence, where he found great pieces of ice littering the shoreline. Sailing into the mouth of the river, he met Micmac Indians who wanted to trade, indicating their desire, as described by historian Peter Hoffer, by "holding up fur pelts on sticks and gesturing the French ashore." Cartier sailed on to Labrador, where some of his men spotted a polar bear and killed it, finding its meat tender and tasty. He passed more Indians, the Beothuks from Newfoundland, hunting seals in the river in birch-bark canoes.

The further west he sailed, the more Cartier became convinced he had reached the mouth of a great river. The sea captain from Breton reached the Magdalen Islands and then modern-day Prince Edward Island. Writing in the mid-twentieth century, historian Thomas Costain describes the beauty of the land Cartier and his men saw before them:

It was a wonderful country. The heat of July had covered the open glades with white and red roses. There were berries and currants in abundance and a wild wheat with ears shaped like barley. The trees were of many familiar kinds, white elm, ash, willow, cedar, and yew. To the north and west were high hills, but these were vastly different from the stern mountains of Newfoundland and the barrenness of the north shore. There was friendliness in their green-covered slopes and a welcome in their approach to the water's edge.

Establishing a Presence

By mid-July Cartier had arrived at Gaspé Harbor, where he encountered another nation of Indians, the Laurentians. He held council with the local chief, Donnaconna, who was, notes historian George MacKinnon Wrong, "clothed in a black bearskin." Their meeting took place in the village of Stadacona, where the French would later establish their community of Quebec. The session with Donnaconna went so well that the chief allowed Cartier to take two of his sons back to France. Perhaps to prepare them for French society, Cartier dressed the chief's sons "in shirts and colored coats, with red caps, putting a copper chain around each of their necks, with which they seemed much pleased."

With storms rising throughout the region he was exploring, Cartier decided it was time to return home. As he departed from the Gulf of St. Lawrence, he was fairly certain he had reached the inlet that would lead him to the Northwest Passage. At Gaspé Harbor the Frenchmen erected a 30-foot (9-meter) Christian cross, along with another piece of wood, inscribed *Vive le Roy de France* ("Long live the king of France").

CARTIER'S SECOND VOYAGE

The "Roy de France" could not have been more pleased with Cartier's success. He ordered a second voyage and three ships for the expedition. In spring the following year the Breton seaman set sail, ready to find the Northwest Passage. He reached the mouth of the river he had explored the previous year on August 10, the feast day of St. Lawrence. To honor the saint, he named the great gulf *La Baye sainct Laurins.*

He intended the name only for the gulf, not the river, but later explorers did not distinguish one from another: Cartier himself called the St. Lawrence *La Grande Rivière* ("the Great River"). At the village of Stadacona, he returned the sons of Chief Donnaconna. The following month Cartier had sailed far enough up the St. Lawrence River to catch a glimpse of rapids in the distance. He was crushed by the realization that the river was not the Northwest Passage. In the meantime he named a local mountain *Mont Royal* ("Mount Royal"), which later gave its name to a French settlement—Montreal.

With the winter season of 1535–36 coming on, Cartier decided on remaining in the region through an exceptionally cold winter, in a fort built near modern-day Quebec. So many of his men became sick with a vitamin deficiency disease called scurvy that there were hardly any fit for guard duty. Only when local Indians told the Frenchmen to boil tea from evergreen tree leaves did the scurvy come under control. Donnaconna told Cartier of a wealthy city called Saguenay which was brimming with gold, jewels, and spices. This caused the French mariner to make a drastic move—he captured the Indian chief and his two sons and took them with him back to France in the spring of 1536, as a way to force their cooperation in finding Saguenay.

SEARCH FOR SAGUENAY

When, after many delays, Cartier returned in 1541 for a third visit to the New World, he reached Chief Donnaconna's village and began searching for Saguenay. But the bejeweled New World city proved to be a fiction, disappointing Cartier and his men. There were other failures. Cartier tried to establish a permanent settlement, but attacks by hostile Iroquois Indians forced him to give up his efforts. The French mariner loaded a large cargo of supposed gold ore and diamonds onto his ships, then discovered on his return to France that the ore was only marcasite and the diamonds only quartz crystals. This third voyage was Cartier's last to the New World. He retired to Saint-Malo, where he died more than 20 years later, in 1557. His voyages had provided France with a legitimate claim to the lands of modern-day Canada, even if the French did not follow them up with serious colonization efforts for another 60 years. As an added complication, the

DESCRIPTION OF THE NEW WORLD

French sea captain René de Laudonnière, who accompanied Jean Ribault on his explorations to Florida in 1562 and 1565, wrote this description of the land, plants, animals, and people, as noted in W. P. Cumming's book, *The Discovery of North America:*

Their woods are full of Oakes, Walnuttrees, blacke Cherrietrees, Mulberry trees, Lentiskes, and Chestnut trees, which are more wilde than those in France. There is great store of Cedars, Cypresses, Bayes, Palme trees, Hollies, and wilde Vines, which climbe up along the trees and beare good Grapes. . . . There are Raspasses [raspberries] *and a little berrie which we call among us Blues, which are very good to eate. . . . There is such abundance of Crocodiles* [alligators]*, that ofentimes in swimming men are assayled by them: of Serpents there are many sorts. There is found amongst the Savages good quantitie of Gold and Silver, which is gotten out of the shippes that are lost upon the coast, as I have understood by the Savages themselves. . . . There is also in this Countrey great store of graynes* [grains] *and herbes, whereof might be made excellent good dyes and paintings of all kindes of colours. And in trueth the Indians which take pleasure in painting of their skins, know very well how to use the same. . . . The most part of them have their bodies, armes, and thighs painted with very faire devises* [designs]*: the painting whereof can never be taken away, because the same is pricked into their flesh.*

English claimed some of the same regions in North America, which resulted in repeated strife and rivalry between these two European nations for years to follow.

THE QUEST FOR GOLD

Cabot, Verrazano, and Cartier had made headway for future English and French colonization in the New World, but all three had failed to meet their other goals of finding the Northwest Passage and finding gold. Treasure mines in Mexico and today's Peru were producing an astonishing amount of gold and silver for the Spanish Crown. During the 1500s the Spanish removed 18,000 tons of silver and 200 tons of gold from New World mines. Galleon after treasure-filled galleon, Spanish vessels sailed through the Straits of Florida, just south of the peninsula of the same name, in a narrow channel flanked by Florida and the Bahaman islands. Eyeing this treasure highway, the French decided to change tactics. Rather than concentrate on establishing colonies far to the North, where gold was almost unknown, they would instead steal gold and silver from the Spanish. To do so, they would need to establish raiding bases along the coast.

CHARLESFORT

The French began to organize their new colony under the leadership of Gaspard de Cologny, a wealthy and influential French Protestant who was also an admiral in the navy. Not wanting the day-to-day responsibilities of running such a colony himself, Cologny delegated much of the job to a career naval officer, Jean Ribault. In the spring of 1562 Ribault sailed to the southern waters of today's United States with three ships and 150 colonists. On May 1 his party, a group of largely French Protestants known as Huguenots, reached Florida's St. John's River, which Ribault claimed for the French king. Taking his party further north, Ribault selected a site for a French colony on the southern end of Port Royal Island, in today's South Carolina. (The site of this colony, known as Charlesfort, would later become the town of Port Royal.)

No sooner had the French landed there and begun the serious work of felling trees for their buildings, then the Europeans began hearing a fresh batch of stories from local Indians about great cities of gold situated just three weeks' walk to the west. The riches the French had not yet discovered in the New World suddenly seemed within grasp. Most of the colonists knew, however, that the key to their survival was not to go off chasing gilded dreams but to work hard to plant their colony and make it last into the future. They also met with local American Indians to establish peaceful relations.

Unsuccessful Attempts

Despite the colonists' efforts, they began to run out of food and ammunition. There were not even enough farm tools to go around. Ribault's answer was to sail back to France for much-needed supplies. Several in the colony chose to give up and go with him, never to return, leaving about 30 colonists at Charlesfort.

Ribault's return to the New World colony was delayed by a French religious war between Catholics and Protestants. The colonists began to argue with one another. Some died from starvation and disease. Those still alive decided to abandon the colony. They built a small boat, using clothing for sails, ready to sail back to France. They left in the spring of 1563, almost a year after the colony was started. Caught out on the high seas without food, the party practiced cannibalism after one of their party died. In this hopeless situation, the last survivors of Charlesfort were fortunate enough to be spotted by an English ship crew, rescued, and taken to London.

RIBAULT RETURNS

The colony at Charlesfort turned out to be an abject failure, but Ribault's first efforts as a colonizer would not be his last. In 1565 Admiral Cologny sent him back to America with seven ships and supplies for another French colony that had been established the previous year along St. John's River in Florida. (This colony occupied the site that would later become the city of Jacksonville, Florida.)

The new French colony, Fort Caroline, had been established as an operational base from which French ships could harass Spanish treasure ships that sailed through the Florida Keys. When the Spanish realized this, they established the site of St. Augustine 50 miles (80 kilometers) to the south. The colony was established by a naval commander, Pedro Menéndez de Avilés, who sailed there from Spain with 1,500 colonists. (St. Augustine is now one of the oldest continually occupied sites in North America, the other being Acoma, the Pueblo Indian site in today's New Mexico.)

INSPIRING THE ENGLISH

In London the survivors of Charlesfort were received by Queen Elizabeth I. In the halls of the English court, the men described the New World as a land of abundant gold, silver, and spices. Their eager English audience even believed their claim of having to mine jewels at night, because they shone too brightly in the daylight.

Driven out of his country by the religious war, Ribault also met with the English queen, and related his own stories of the opportunities waiting in America. He even published a book in 1563, *The Whole and True Discovery of Terra Florida*, which was enthusiastically read across the length and breadth of England. His glowing account and the tales told by the Charlesfort survivors fired the imaginations of a new generation of English adventurers.

SURPRISE ATTACK

Menéndez wasted little time mounting an expedition to march on Fort Caroline. His men pushed their way up the coast through three days of torrential rains. Their attack on the French fort caught the French completely off-guard. (At the time of the attack, Ribault was absent.) The battle lasted less than an hour, and most of the French were killed on the spot, 140 men in all. Approximately 60 women and children were spared. Others, however, escaped and lived to return to France and report what had taken place.

Ribault was to lead a retaliatory attack against St. Augustine, but a hurricane struck his ship on the way, leaving him and several hundred men stranded on a Caribbean island. Later they were discovered by Menéndez, whose soldiers slaughtered almost all of them, including Ribault, sparing only the lives of two French Catholics. (The Spanish had been ordered by King Philip II not to execute Catholics, English or not.) With the losses of both Charlesfort and Fort Caroline, the French were discouraged from establishing any other colonies in the New World for the remainder of the 1500s.

2

England Tries Its Hand

Throughout the final decades of the 1500s the French and Spanish engaged in a sometimes brutal competition for dominance in the New World. Their clashes took place not only in Florida, but from Hudson Bay to Brazil. Sometimes their confrontations devolved into little more than retaliatory raids, such as the two that Menéndez carried out against Ribault and the colonists at Fort Caroline. Incidentally, Menéndez's massacre of Ribault and hundreds of Frenchmen in 1565 was avenged three years later when a French pirate, Dominique de Gourgues, attacked the Spanish who had taken over Fort Caroline and murdered all his prisoners.

ENGLAND ENTERS THE GAME

Several factors kept the English from entering this sometimes deadly competition during the latter decades of the 1500s. The English could not match the might of the Spanish navy, or Spanish Armada, which plied the high seas from the Mediterranean to the New World. Its presence kept English ships far to the North, away from Florida and the Caribbean. Even then the English only established temporary fishing villages off the Canadian coasts of Newfoundland, just as the French had already done. Here they caught cod and traded everything from mirrors to hammers with the Indians.

By the late 1500s, however, a handful of brave English sea captains were ready to challenge Spanish supremacy in the New World. Some, such as Sir Humphrey Gilbert and Sir Walter Raleigh, attempted to establish colonies. Others, such as John Hawkins and Francis Drake, raided Spanish treasure ships, just as the French had already done. Hawkins began raiding after Spanish officials in the Caribbean banned him from trading in their colonies. The Spanish even engaged Hawkins in a battle on the high seas, a fight that cost him three of his five ships. (The two surviving ships were captained by Hawkins and his cousin Francis Drake.)

In 1577 Queen Elizabeth sent Francis Drake to campaign against the Spanish in the New World. (Relations between the English queen, who supported the Protestants, and Philip II of Spain, who was staunchly Catholic, had deteriorated.) Armed with six ships, Drake raided Spanish coastal communities, sailed around the southern tip of South America, and harassed Spanish settlements in Chile and Peru. Along the way he attacked Spanish treasure vessels. Drake returned home the hard way, via the vast Pacific Ocean, in order to avoid capture by the Spanish.

FURTHER ENGLISH EXPLORATIONS

The exploits of Drake and Hawkins gained them both knighthoods, but did not bring England any nearer to establishing colonies in the New World. Those efforts fell to others, such as the courtier Sir Humphrey Gilbert. Like the French before him, Gilbert believed the way to meet the challenge Spain represented in the New World was to build a line of forts north of New Spain. He hoped to block the Spanish from moving any further north than the old Fort Caroline site, which the Spanish had renamed Fort San Mateo.

To encourage support for his colonial ventures, Gilbert wrote *Discourse of a Discovery for a New Passage to Catia* [Cathay, or China], which he published in the 1570s. In the book, Gilbert argued that the Northwest Passage was still to be discovered and that English colonizers could convert the American Indians to Protestantism. Suggesting that he might lead the way if adequately sponsored, Gilbert stated he wanted nothing from his efforts but to keep any treasure he personally discovered in the New World. Queen Elizabeth responded by financing several exploratory voyages.

FROBISHER SETS SAIL

Although Gilbert had written boldly about England's potential to colonize in North America, he did not go himself. He hired a skilled English sea captain, Martin Frobisher, to make the first Elizabeth-sponsored voyage, in 1576. With the Northwest Passage as his primary goal, Frobisher traveled further north than any previous explorer of his time. Sailing north of the 50th parallel, he found himself one day facing a sudden storm, of which Frobisher wrote, as noted by historian Peter Hoffer, "the ice came upon us so fast, we were in great danger, looking every hour for death." With ice hanging from the masts and ship's rigging, the crewmen whacked icicles with oars and long wooden staves. But the icy world also impressed Frobisher with its beauty: "and thus we lay off and on we came by a marvelous huge mountain of ice, which surpassed all the rest that we saw . . . being there nine score fathoms deepe, and of compass about half a mile."

The Northwest Passage itself remained elusive. Frobisher also searched for gold, picking up huge quantities of metal on Baffin Island, which he believed was gold. (It proved to be worthless iron pyrite, or fool's gold.) He made second and third voyages in 1577 and 1578, but still no northern route to China was found. On his second effort, he collected a thousand tons of ore, again hoping it was gold, and again being fooled by iron pyrite.

GILBERT'S VOYAGE

Disappointed by Frobisher's three voyages, Gilbert decided to sail in search of the Northwest Passage himself. In 1578 he set off with a fleet of seven ships and combined crew of 400 men. Violent storms prevented him from reaching America, so he tried again five years later, even using some of his family fortune to help fund the venture.

Gilbert landed at the port of St. John's, Newfoundland, but storms struck soon afterward and his ship was lost at sea. Sir Humphrey Gilbert's dreams of New World treasure did not die with him, however. A new English entrepreneur stepped forward to take his place: Sir Walter Raleigh, Gilbert's half-brother.

RALEIGH SENDS A SCOUTING PARTY

Gilbert and Raleigh were similar to one another in outlook, attitude, and beliefs. Both loyally supported Queen Elizabeth and had the inside track in the English court. Both had fought to force Protestantism on Catholic Ireland. In Ireland, however, Raleigh had made trouble for himself. When he ordered the hangings of a dozen Catholic women, several of whom were pregnant, as well as the deaths of hundreds of prisoners of war, his actions led to the denial of a land grant in Ireland. In need of land and money, Raleigh was driven to request his brother's patent, or right, to establish a New World colony. Despite his excesses in Ireland, Elizabeth granted him the privilege.

In 1584 Raleigh dispatched a group of men to North America to scout out the lands. In late spring two English ships landed first on the Caribbean island of Puerto Rico, then sailed north, reached modern-day North Carolina, and made contact with the Roanoke Indians, who lived on an island off the mainland.

When the English ships dropped anchor off the island, the party made preparations, and, as noted by historian Allen

A scene showing Arawak Indians on the island of Hispaniola, which is today occupied by Haiti and the Dominican Republic. It was drawn by a Frenchman on Francis Drake's voyage to the West Indies in 1585.

Weinstein, "after thanks given to God for our safe arrival hither, we manned our boats and went to view the land . . . and to take possession of the same, in the right of the Queen's most excellent Majesty." The land appeared good, supporting plenty of game, and the Europeans noted the "sweet and aromatic smells [that] lay in the air." The party was immediately impressed by the local Indians, meeting with the chief, Wingina. When this advance group returned to England, they encouraged Raleigh to establish his colony on Roanoke Island. They even brought back with them two Indian youths, Manteo and Wanchese. To encourage Queen Elizabeth in her support of the venture, Raleigh chose to name his future colony *Virginia,* after the "Virgin Queen." (Elizabeth had never married.)

RALEIGH'S FIRST COLONY

A year later Raleigh sent his 100-man-strong colonizing party off to America, onboard seven ships, calling them, as noted by historian James Horn, "a remarkable group of men who brought together scientific knowledge and practical experience." (Raleigh had hoped for 800 colonists. He had also intended to go to America with them, but the queen did not want him to leave.) Among their number was a mathematician and scientist trained at Oxford University, Thomas Harriot, as well as a young artist, John White. Another member was a Jewish mineralogist, Joachim Ganz, whose duty it was to search for gold and silver. (In the early 1990s archaeologists excavating at Roanoke found the remains of a metallurgical laboratory, including pieces of ceramic, Bohemian glass, and copper. Perhaps these were the remains of Ganz's equipment.) The colonists also included soldiers, carpenters, farmers, winemakers, and druggists.

The colony's first efforts did not bear fruit. They built a fort and even included a row of craft shops, like a street in a small English village. However, since the shops had no real customers, that part of the settlement was a failure. The group also found neither gold nor silver. Food became a problem, since they reached Roanoke too late in the season to grow crops. At first they received food from the local Indians but when they continued to rely on these handouts, the Indian tribal leader, Wingina, cut off this food source. Stupidly, the colony's military leader, Captain Ralph Lane, attacked a local Indian village and killed the chief of the Roanokes. This caused a permanent break between the English and the Indians. Things turned from bad to worse. A year later, with many colonists starving, Francis Drake chanced by and picked them up. Raleigh's first attempt at a colony had collapsed.

RALEIGH TRIES AGAIN

In 1587 Raleigh organized a second colonizing party, and managed to get 150 colonists to sign up for the venture, including artist John White. White and Harriot had written a short book since their return, *Brief and True Report of the New Found Land of Virginia,* which White had illustrated, and this had helped recruit the new batch of colonists, who this time included women and children as well as men. (Two of the women were even pregnant.) Raleigh had high hopes for this effort, and he decided to name the settlement site after himself—"The City of Raleigh in the Colony of Virginia." He even had a special coat of arms commissioned for his American "city."

The colonists reached America in April. They did not land at the same site as the earlier colony, but established themselves on the north end of Roanoke Island, in the region of Chesapeake Bay. No sooner had the colonists landed, their ship's captain, Simon Fernandez, left them, sailing south to raid Spanish treasure ships. Again, they arrived too late to

THE MYSTERY OF ROANOKE

In 1590 John White's ship reached Roanoke Island in the dark of night. White later wrote in his journal, as noted by historian Allen Weinstein, "We let fall our Grapnel [anchor] neere the shore & sounded with a trumpet a Call, & afterward many familiar English tunes of Songs, and called to them friendly; but we had no answere."

White found the colony abandoned. Everyone was gone, including his daughter, son-in-law, and granddaughter. The site was a clutter of discarded items, including books and small furniture. On a nearby tree, someone had left behind a tantalizing clue—the three letters C R O. Perhaps it was meant as a message, that the colonists were forced by circumstances to leave their settlement and take refuge with the Croatoan tribe whose village was only 50 miles (80 kilometers) southwest on a neighboring island.

No one knows what happened to the colonists. In time, history would record Raleigh's second effort to set up an English presence in the New World as the Lost Colony of Roanoke.

English settlers sent by Walter Raleigh arrived at Roanoke Island in 1585 and set up the colony.

raise their own food, spent too much time looking for gold, and ran out of supplies. Their leader John White agreed to return to England for more supplies, and left as soon as his daughter, Elinor Dare, gave birth to his granddaughter, Virginia. (Virginia was the first English child born in the New World.)

All the colony's hopes hung on White's return. Unfortunately, the timing could not have been worse. England was at war with Spain and, threatened by the might of the Spanish Armada, no ship was allowed to leave England, including White's. White was not able to return to Roanoke until 1590, three years after he had left—and by then, the colony had been abandoned.

3
Jamestown

When Raleigh received the news of the Lost Colony of Roanoke, it did not change his mind about supporting colonies in the New World. He had already decided to give up on such efforts, realizing that they did not translate into instant riches. In 1589 Raleigh had transferred his patent to colonize "Virginia" to an investment group of 19 wealthy individuals, including several London merchants. But these men did not jump into the colonizing business. No one understood their reluctance more than Raleigh.

THE POPHAM COLONY

A new century brought new English adventurers to America. In 1602 English merchants and traders began making their way to the New World, not to Roanoke, but to the north, to modern-day Massachusetts and Maine. At first, they did not settle, but came over to trade animal furs with the Indians and to cut cedar trees for the English market. The English efforts in the New World were largely private enterprises, without direct financial help from either Queen Elizabeth or, after her death in 1603, from King James I.

In 1606 a group of English merchants sent a party of explorers and colonizers to the New World. They were part of the Plymouth Company, a joint-stock venture, which had been given the rights to colonize anywhere they could between Maine and modern-day Virginia's Potomac River. As a joint-stock company, these investors raised their own capital by buying stock in the company and by selling stock to others. The money raised allowed company officials to buy the needed ships and supplies, as well as recruit colonists.

The expedition established its settlement site on a peninsula at the mouth of the Kennebec River, in today's Maine. (The local Indians called the river the Sagadahoc.) Since one of the colony's leading supporters was England's chief justice, Sir John Popham, the settlement was named the Popham Colony. The leader of the group was Martin Pring, who selected the site for the colony. One of the first things the colonists did was construct a fort and trading post. The following year, 40 men arrived as colonists, led by George Popham, one of Sir John's relatives, and Raleigh Gilbert, 24-year-old son of Sir Humphrey.

The colony struggled through its first winter, during which George Popham died, and a fire engulfed the store-room where most of the colony's supplies were kept. In addition, Indian relations reached a low point. With half the colony's members dead by spring of 1608, the colonists cobbled together a small, 30-ton ship and sailed back to England. At the time, they were unaware that another group of English colonists had already established themselves further south, at the mouth of the Chesapeake River, in a settlement site they called Fort James, and which was very soon known as Jamestown.

FOUNDING JAMESTOWN

Meanwhile, another group of investors had formed the London (or Virginia) Company in 1606 and received a grant to colonize further south, from the mouth of the Hudson River (where New York City is located today) to North Carolina. Its land grant charters overlapped with those of the Plymouth Company between the Hudson and Potomac rivers.

In late 1606 the colonists left England for Virginia on three small ships, including the 120-ton *Susan Constant,* the 40-ton *Godspeed,* and the 20-ton pinnace, *Discovery.* (The smallest boat was intended for use up the various rivers in the colony's region.) They comprised 140 men and four boys as well as crew members, and included common laborers, bricklayers, soldiers, and goldsmiths, plus a surgeon, blacksmith, carpenter, barber, minister, perfumer, and a tailor.

Aware they would encounter Indians in America, the company had hired a military leader named John Smith, whose contributions to the colony would prove greatly important. (Smith was so certain of himself that during the voyage he insulted the colony's leaders, calling them incompetent, which landed him in the brig, slated for execution for insubordination. Fortunately, the sentence was never carried out.) After a difficult sea voyage, the ships reached the coast of modern-day Virginia on April 26, 1607. They began to search for a suitable site for their fort—a place along a river narrow enough that their cannon could hit an enemy ship, such as the Spanish, in mid-stream, and wide enough to allow oceangoing trade vessels to reach the site.

Captain Christopher Newport, one of the most capable sea mariners of his time, selected a potato-shaped peninsula along a river the party named the James, after their monarch. The site was covered with trees and meadows and was located 50 miles (80 kilometers) upriver from Chesapeake Bay, out of sight of Spanish ships that might run the coastline.

DIFFICULTIES AT JAMESTOWN

It did not take long before it became clear that James Island was not a good site. There was plenty of land, 800 acres (325 hectares) in all, but much of it was swampy, and mosquitoes proved a continuous problem. (No one then understood, however, that mosquitoes transmitted malaria, yet another problem at Fort James.) The groundwater on the peninsula was mixed with seawater, and the ground tended to hold nearly all the human waste produced by the colonists. Drinking and washing clothes in polluted water spread even more disease, including typhoid and dysentery. In short order, men began dying at the rate of one or two almost daily. Things began to look no better for the men of Fort James than they had proven for the English colonists at Popham Colony.

Other problems plagued the English outpost. Food was scarce, since the men had eaten more of their supplies on the voyage than they expected. They came intending to experiment with such crops as melons, cotton, potatoes, and even orange trees, but they did not sow many plants for food production. Class differences caused problems among the population. The upper-class gentlemen did not expect to perform manual labor in the colony, since such men did not work back in England. Precious manpower was wasted in fruitless quests for gold. Local Indians also proved difficult. The closest nation, the Paspahegh, were part of an Indian alliance known as Powhatan's Confederation. The Paspahegh claimed James Island and, when a scouting party of colonists explored further upriver and gave gifts to a rival tribe, the Paspahegh attacked the fort.

Despite these difficulties, the men at Jamestown marveled at the land they were trying to turn into their home. John Smith wrote in his *Generall Historie of Virginia,* "All the country is overgrowne with trees. The wood that is most common is Oke and Walnut: many of their Okes are so tall and

straight, that they will beare two foot and a half of good timber for 20 yards long." Colonists' writings list the abundant
wildlife, and mention such oddities as the opossum which
William Strachey, the colony's secretary, observed, as noted
by historian W. P. Cumming, "is a beast as big as a pretty
Beagle of grey cullor, yt hath a head like a swine, eares, Feet,
and Taile like a Ratt . . . and eats [tastes] like a Pig."

Smith noted the rich local marine life: "In sommer, no
place affordeth more plenty of Sturgeon, nor in Winter more
abundance of fowle, especially in time of frost. . . . The oyster
beds rimmed the banks of the tidal rivers and proved later to
be one of the easiest and most certain sources of food in time
of scarcity." In some oysters, the colonists found pearls.

Following the fire at Jamestown, the colonists built
sturdy houses and buildings with wood frames, and
a protective wood fence. This reconstruction of the
fort is next to the site of the original settlement.

From May to August a long, hot summer of difficulties and death left Jamestown with only five or six inhabitants fit to work. By January 1608 only 38 men remained alive. Fortunately, Captain Newport, who had left the colony for England, returned with supplies and 120 new colonists. Food was available for all. Only five days after Newport's return, however, a fire destroyed nearly all the buildings in the fort, including the storehouse of ammunition and supplies. Only three buildings remained, and the colonists soon faced Jamestown's coldest months of winter yet.

Jamestown and its miserable residents might have failed totally were it not for the skillful leadership of John Smith. Although Smith was not among the appointed leaders of the colony, the men respected him. He brought discipline to the group, informing them all, commoner and gentleman alike, that anyone who did not work would not be provided with food. Some colonists plotted to leave the colony and return to England, but when Smith found out, he ordered the arrest of the ringleader, who was tried for treason and shot.

Smith took additional steps to see to the welfare of the colonists. He sent out foraging parties to find food. He made contact with local Indians and managed to get food from them. In the spring of 1609, Newport returned a third time and brought 70 new recruits, including eight Poles and Germans, some expert glassmakers. The colony Newport saw was much improved. A new and cleaner well had been excavated, 20 new buildings had been constructed, and the rate of deaths had slowed considerably. The colony appeared destined for survival, to the credit of Captain John Smith.

THE "STARVING TIME"

After two years of colonizing, many of Jamestown's early problems seemed to have been conquered or smoothed over. That stability came at a high price. Of the first 300 colonists to settle at Fort James, known within months as Jamestown, only 80 lived to see the summer of 1609, a survival rate of just over 25 percent. That same summer, the colony received 400 new colonists onboard seven ships. (Two earlier vessels failed to reach Jamestown, one lost at sea and the other shipwrecked on the island of Bermuda.) When they arrived, they discovered the colony in near chaos. Food was in short

STORIES OF JOHN SMITH

Only 26 years old when the Jamestown colonists set sail from England, John Smith was already a veteran soldier. He had inherited his father's Lincolnshire farm at age 17, but chose instead to travel to Europe and hire himself out as a mercenary to fight the advancing Ottoman Turks. He soon made the rank of captain.

In 1602 Smith was captured in Romania and sold as a slave in Constantinople. According to his autobiography, Smith killed his owner and escaped with the help of a beautiful princess. In another story, he cut off the head of the best fighter in the Turkish army in one-on-one combat.

Smith did not look much like a great warrior—he was short, even compared to men of his day, and had a bright red, fan-shaped beard—but he had confidence, and did not balk at telling his stories to anyone who would listen.

As Fort James's military leader, Smith often explored the region around the English colony and negotiated with Indians for supplies. One of his most famous stories tells how Indians took him prisoner and brought him before their chief, Powhatan. A warrior was about to club him to death when he was saved by the chief's daughter, Pocahontas. Smith wrote in his *Generall Historie of Virginia* (1624): "Pocahontas, the king's daughter, when no entreaty would prevail, got [my] head in her arms and laid her own upon [mine] to save [me] from death." Historians wonder about the truth of Smith's exciting tale, but today the story is told and retold without question.

supply again and housing was limited. John Smith was no longer able to provide adequate leadership. A careless sailor dropped pipe ash on Smith's powder flask while he lay sleeping and the resulting gunpowder explosion left Smith with serious wounds that forced his removal back to England. (Smith would return in 1614 to map and name New England and "Plimouth," the land opposite Cape Cod.)

With Smith gone and the winter of 1609–10 approaching, the colonists settled in for a difficult season. There was little actual leadership in Fort James, food was short, and death stalked the colony. In addition, local Indians turned on the

Pocahontas (standing) asks her father, Powhatan, (seated) to spare the life of John Smith. From Smith's *Generall Historie of Virginia*.

settlers, besieged the fort, and killed all stray English live-stock. The colonists soon slipped into a twilight world that would be remembered later as the "Starving Time." In his *Generall Historie,* John Smith described the 60 (out of nearly 500) who survived as "most miserable and poore creatures . . . preserved for the most part, by roots, herbes, acorns, walnuts, berries, now and then a little fish." They had also eaten dogs, cats, rats, snakes, toadstools, and horsehides. In the later stages of those miserable months, they ate "one another [boiled] and stewed with roots and herbs." When it was discovered that one man had killed his wife, salted her body to preserve it like a piece of meat, and eaten her corpse, colonists burned him to death.

EXPANSION

The winter of 1609–1610 proved to be the low point in the early years of the Jamestown colony. Only by establishing military rule did colonial leaders gain control of the situations that plagued the settlement. One decision was for the colonists not to remain contained in Jamestown, but to spread out up and down the James River and beyond. They built other fortified villages, planting local fields with corn, peas, and barley. Food issues, in time, became a concern of the past. Women were introduced into the all-male colony in 1609, families formed, and children soon followed. (Men continued to outnumber women until the turn of the century, though.) Death was never far away, however; between 1619 and 1622, the Virginia Company delivered nearly 3,600 colonists to the outpost. Throughout those same three years, 3,000 of them—more than 80 percent—died.

IMPROVEMENTS IN JAMESTOWN

One crucial improvement was the introduction of a new cash crop: tobacco. A settler named John Rolfe (who later married the famed Indian girl, Pocahontas) found the local "Indian tobacco," to be harsh, scarce, and costly. As he described it, according to historian Allen Weinstein, locally grown tobacco was "poore and weake, and of a biting taste."

Rolfe became desperate for good tobacco, which he knew grew in the Caribbean. He introduced a Caribbean variety

A COLONY GOES UP IN SMOKE

When Christopher Columbus had landed in the New World in 1492, he discovered Indians on the island of Cuba smoking small "cigars." He had brought tobacco back to Europe and it was soon all the rage. Sir Walter Raleigh had popularized smoking in England during the 1580s—but it was not popular with everyone. In 1604 King James I, according to historian Allen Weinstein, described the pastime as "a custom loathsome to the eye, hateful to the nose, harmful to the brain, dangerous to the lungs, and in the black stinking fume thereof, nearest resembling the horrible Stygian smoke of the pit that is bottomless." (The king was comparing tobacco smoke to the vapors of hell!)

Part of the king's concern may have been that all tobacco came from Spanish-owned plantations.

By introducing Caribbean tobacco to Jamestown, John Rolfe gave the English a share of the market. He sent his first shipment back to England in 1613. Soon, others in Virginia began growing tobacco—in fact, so much land was given over to the crop that there was not enough corn being raised to feed the colonists.

Tobacco became such an important part of the economy that it was sometimes exchanged instead of money. Taxes were occasionally paid in tobacco. In 1619 a shipload of women arrived at Jamestown and the men of the settlement could "buy" a wife for 120 pounds (55 kilograms) of tobacco—the cost of her ship passage. By bringing tobacco to Virginia and helping to establish it as a crop, Rolfe had helped pave the way not only for the colony's survival, but for its prosperity as well.

of tobacco to Virginia, and discovered that air-drying helped keep the flavor sweet and full. In 1616 Virginians exported 2,500 pounds (1,130 kilograms) of tobacco. By 1619 colonists in the region of Jamestown produced 40,000 pounds (18,150 kg) of tobacco for export. Just 10 years later, Virginia tobacco exports had skyrocketed to 1.5 million pounds (680,400 kg)! After decades of difficulty, desolation, and death, Jamestown residents finally began to prosper.

There were other improvements, too. In 1618 the Virginia Company changed its land policy. Previously, all land occupied by the colonists still belonged to the company and was farmed as common land. But that year company officials agreed to hand out land grants of 100 acres (40.5 hectares) each to all colonists who had lived in the colony since 1607. Any colonists arriving after 1618 would receive 50 acres (20.25 ha) of land, once they had paid their ship passage to the New World. This system, called the "headright system," suddenly put land into the hands of hundreds, and later thousands, of English immigrants.

The following year, 1619, saw more positive change as the first elected legislature in North America began meeting. This early body was called the House of Burgesses, with two representatives, or burgesses, elected from each of the 11 regions of the Virginia colony. Virginia's government now included a governor, who was appointed in England and served for life; a council of advisors, whose members were appointed by the governor; and an elected legislature. For the first time the colonists could pass their own laws and, at least in part, govern their own world.

4

Religious Freedom and the Pilgrims

Not until a generation had passed following the establishment of Jamestown in 1607 did the colony stabilize and prosper. By that time a new group of colonizers were laying the groundwork for a new type of colony, just to the north of Jamestown and Virginia. While Jamestown had been the work of a joint-stock company, this new venture was led by one man, an English Catholic named George Calvert, also known as Lord Baltimore.

When his political career was cut short due to his religion, George Calvert made the decision to leave England for the New World. King Charles I, who was sympathetic to Catholics such as Calvert, agreed to grant Calvert a colony in a region of North America that was already established and prospering—the Tidewater Region, which included Jamestown and Virginia.

Calvert's land grant was huge, consisting of 10 million acres (4 million hectares) of American land, which bordered on the northern and eastern shores of Chesapeake Bay. The grant represented new hope for Calvert. But he died at the age of 52, leaving the opportunities of his new colony to his family. One of Calvert's sons, Cecilius Calvert, soon received the grant and was named Lord Proprietor of Maryland, which the family named after Charles I's wife, Queen Henrietta Maria.

MARYLAND

Although Cecilius received the grant, he stayed in England and appointed one of his brothers, Leonard Calvert, to take the leadership for the family. By 1633 arrangements had been made for two ships, the *Ark* and the *Dove,* to carry 250 people to the Maryland colony. The Calverts had advertised their colony as a safe haven for fellow Catholics, so approximately half of the first group of colonists were Catholics. (Those who were not members of the Church of England were sometimes persecuted in England.) The ships left England in December and arrived in the Chesapeake region by February 1634.

The party established a settlement called St. Mary's, where they found the land rich for farming. Taking Virginia as their example, they based their colony's economy on tobacco production. Soon, tobacco fields dotted the Maryland landscape, where one field hand could plant and tend as many as 6,000 tobacco plants annually. This allowed the colonists to avoid some of the hardships endured by the Jamestown settlers. In some cases the colonists did not even have to clear their land of trees, since Indians had done much of the work when they had lived there years earlier.

The Maryland colony was not without problems, however. With both Catholics and Protestants living side by side, conflicts arose, leading to the passage of a Maryland law called the Act of Toleration (1649) which guaranteed all Marylanders who were Christians the right to worship as they chose.

THE DUTCH SEND HUDSON

While much of the New World exploration was carried out by the larger, more powerful European states—England, Spain, France—some smaller states added their involvement, and sometimes the results proved significant. One such country was the sea-bound state of Holland, or the Netherlands.

In 1602 the Dutch established a giant, global trading firm, the East India Company. Primarily founded to coordinate trade in the Far East, the company became an important rival of the Spanish and Portuguese. In an effort to avoid contact with either power in the normal sea lanes around Africa, the Dutch offered a cash prize to any sea captain who could find an alternate route, either north of Europe or through the fabled Northwest Passage. To that end, an English sailor named Henry Hudson contracted with the Dutch East India in January 1609 to find such a passage.

By the summer of 1609, Hudson had reached modern-day Canada and begun his explorations. He moved his ship, the *Half Moon*, along the coast of Maine, which had already been explored, and was approached by a canoe of Penobscot Indians, ready to trade. Hudson continued on, sailing south to modern-day Virginia, near Jamestown, and then north to the site of today's New York City, at the mouth of the river that would one day be named for Hudson. Curious, he sailed up the river to the place where Albany, New York, is located today. Perhaps he had found the Northwest Passage, thought Hudson. But, immediately north of the confluence of the Mohawk and Hudson rivers, the channel narrowed, indicating to Hudson that he was pursuing a false lead.

When he sailed back east, Hudson first stopped in England, sending his report ahead. In it, he suggested several sites along the Hudson River for possible trading posts and a permanent Dutch colony. (A few years later the Dutch did establish a colony in the region, which they called New Netherland.)

THE HUDSON'S BAY COMPANY

English merchants followed up Henry Hudson's explorations by establishing the Hudson's Bay Company, a New World venture whose purpose was to trade furs with the Indians. It proved profitable from the beginning, and the company still exists today. The Dutch also followed up on Hudson's voyage to America by building a trading post on an island in the Hudson River near modern-day Albany, which they called Fort Orange, after Holland's royal family.

This single outpost was only the beginning of Dutch colonizing efforts in North America. They also positioned themselves for business with the Indians at the mouth of the Delaware River, along the Hudson River, including on an island then occupied by the Manhattan Indians (known today as Manhattan Island). A decade after Hudson's voyag-

HUDSON'S LAST VOYAGE

In 1610 Hudson set off for North America again, this time exploring for a group of English merchants. He sailed north to avoid contact with French settlements and trading posts and discovered a great bay, which would come to be named after him. It was there that Hudson and his crew became trapped by ice. Tiring of Hudson's stubbornness and arrogance, his crew mutinied. Hudson, his son, and a handful of sailors were left in a small boat in the bay, as the mutineers set sail for England. Although the London merchants sent a rescue ship, Hudson and his loyal crewmen were never found, and their fate is unknown to this day.

es to the New World, the Dutch established the Dutch West India Company. Some of the company's efforts were focused on engaging in the New World slave trade and in Brazil, but they also invested in New Netherland, sending the company's first colonists to settle on Manhattan Island in 1623.

By 1625 the Dutch in New Amsterdam (modern-day New York City) had built a trading post, fort, windmill, and a defensive wall, a portion of which became known as Wall

The earliest known view of New Amsterdam, from an engraving dated 1626–1628 by Dutchman Joost Hartgers. It shows Indian canoes, colonists' sailing ships, and a settlement at the tip of Manhattan Island.

Street. By 1626, after a few years of hugging the southern tip of Manhattan, Dutch colonial governor Pieter Minuit is said to have purchased the whole island from a local Indian clan, for 60 guilders (approximately $24). (If the transaction ever took place, it is unlikely that the local Indians actually thought they were selling the island and their rights to it.) Fifteen years following the explorations of Henry Hudson, the Dutch were firmly positioned in the New World, especially North America.

SPAIN AND THE SOUTHWEST

While much of the North American colonizing of the 1600s took place along the Atlantic seaboard, from Florida to Newfoundland, other parts of the continent also saw the establishment of new colonies. The Spanish had been the first colonizers of the Americas following Columbus's arrival in the New World, but most of their colonies stretched from the Caribbean to Mexico to South America.

In 1598, one of the earliest of these Spanish adventurers was dispatched to New Mexico. He was Juan de Onate, whose family had become wealthy from New World mining. Granted permission to establish a colony, Onate took a party of 400 people, including 130 soldiers and their families, a band of Indians, and 20 Franciscan padres with him. Onate was serious about his colony. He had put up the money for the entire venture.

He and his colonists marched north from Mexico City across the bleak landscape of northern Mexico, until they reached the upper Rio Grande Valley in modern-day north-central New Mexico. He reached the Pueblo village of the Acoma, who occupied the heights of a 350-foot-tall (105-meter) mesa called Sky City. When the Spanish party approached, the Acoma were not friendly. Rather than skirt around the pueblo village, Onate stubbornly chose to lay siege, with the Indians throwing down rocks from the heights above. In time, the Spanish reached the top of the mesa and killed 800 men, women, and children. Onate also ordered his men to cut off one foot of each of the surviving male Indians. Several in his party were appalled by Onate's decision to attack the Acoma, and the news eventually reached officials back in

EARLY SPANISH COLONIZATION

The Spanish had made some effort to colonize Florida, but they had largely left North America alone. After Francisco Coronado had reached the Southwest during the 1540s, the door had been opened for further and future Spanish colonization in North America.

Coronado had explored the Southwest from California to New Mexico. Despite Coronado's efforts, however, Spain did not immediately follow up with new colonies in the region. Coronado's expedition had failed to find any significant wealth or the Seven Golden Cities of Cibola (which did not exist), so the Spanish had, at first, written off the wilderness, desert region. But by the 1580s a new group of Spanish adventurers, Franciscan missionaries, had returned to the lands Coronado had explored 40 years earlier. They entered New Mexico not in search of gold and wealth, but to save the souls of Indians, whom they thought needed Christ and salvation.

These Catholic missionaries were not always well received and some were hounded out and even killed by the Indians. Others, however, were accepted and Spain regained a toehold in the northern provinces of Mexico.

The Franciscans may not have entered the Southwest searching for treasure, but they constantly heard stories of vast wealth to the north— stories of gold and silver mines along the banks of the middle region of the Rio Grande. When the padres retold these tales to Spanish officials in Mexico City, the Spanish viceroy decided to send colonists into the region, some of whom could look for the lost golden cities once more.

Mexico City. They ordered Onate to return, stripped him of his aristocratic titles, and banned him from reentering New Mexico.

In 1609, when Jamestown colonists were in the midst of their "Starving Time," Spanish leaders sent a new colonizing party into the region. They were to give support to the Catholic missionaries who were already there and make New Mexico into a special missionary colony. The newly appointed governor was Don Pedro de Peralta, who reached New Mexico in 1610. Peralta would soon establish a new Spanish community in the lands of the Pueblo Indians: Santa Fe (meaning "Holy Faith"). This new outpost would become the first permanent European colony in the Spanish Southwest.

THE FRENCH MOVE INLAND

Following the French removal from modern-day Florida and Georgia during the 1560s, there was little follow up in North America by later French explorers or colonial organizers. But the French could not remain out of the New World game forever. With Spain, England, Portugal, and even Holland establishing colonies from Hudson Bay to the Straits of Magellan, the French resurrected their interest and old claims to the New World.

In 1603 Henry IV of France dispatched Samuel de Champlain to the Gulf of St. Lawrence to establish an outpost where furs could be traded with the local Indians. In 1608 Champlain returned to Canada with another group of French colonists and founded the trading station at Quebec. From that base, he explored for hundreds of miles to the south and west, down through modern-day New York state to the lake that would be named for him. By 1612, after several years in the region of the upper St. Lawrence River, Champlain had established friendly relations with the Indians and smoothed the way for further French activity. Moving further west, he explored the lands of the Great Lakes.

As the decades passed, the French consolidated their presence in today's Canada, even as the pace of their colonization remained slow and sometimes methodical. The 1670s saw the next great French explorer in the region of the St. Lawrence River—René-Robert Cavelier de La Salle. La Salle even explored the Mississippi River where he reached its mouth at the Gulf of Mexico, half a continent to the south of the Great Lakes. The whole country that today makes up much of the Great Plains was claimed by La Salle in the name of the French monarch, Louis XIV.

THE PILGRIMS

The history of the people remembered as the Pilgrims began following the 1534 separation of England from the Roman Catholic Church. For his own reasons, King Henry VIII encouraged the establishment of the Church of England, with himself as its head. This significant step was taken as part of the greater historical movement that swept across Europe during the 1500s, the Protestant Reformation. Those who did not believe that Catholicism and its teachings reflected true Christianity chose to separate themselves from the Church and establish their own faith traditions. In England, Henry VIII made this split for his people. Among English Protestants were Anabaptists—a radical group—and a sect that wanted to purify the Anglican Church's practices, who were commonly called "Puritans." The Puritans sought to make the religious practices of the Anglican Church much less Catholic in form. They did not believe an official priesthood was necessary, but wanted to interpret the Bible for themselves. They wanted a church that was less formal, and sought simplicity in everything, including their lifestyles, which did not include such "worldly" distractions as dancing, attending the theater, or celebrating Christmas. Honest work and plain religion were their goals.

In time, many Puritans came to believe that changing the Church of England was not possible. They abandoned Anglicanism, calling themselves "Separatists." Because they did not support the official English church, the Separatists were sometimes persecuted, with the king's soldiers breaking up their meetings and arresting their leaders. This led one group of Separatists, a congregation in the town of Scrooby in Nottinghamshire, to leave England altogether and move to Holland, where they could practice their religious beliefs without interference. But their stay in Holland did not prove successful. The Separatists had gained religious freedom but they felt the Dutch were too worldly. It was difficult to find well-paid labor, and the Separatists' children began speaking Dutch and marrying Dutch spouses.

After some of the Separatists' leaders began reading Captain John Smith's published descriptions of America, they considered moving to the New World, where they could create a whole new society from top to bottom, with no interferences or distractions to draw them away from their faith. Perhaps Smith's "New England" might just be the answer. Plans were made with a merchant company in London and, after 10 frustrating years in Leiden, 35 Separatists packed up and sailed to the New World in the fall of 1620, onboard an aging wine vessel named the *Mayflower*.

After a harrowing voyage, the *Mayflower*'s 102 passengers reached the shores of New England's Cape Cod. (During the sail across the Atlantic, one member of the party died and a baby was born, keeping the number at 102.) As storms had pushed their ship further north than the colonists had intended to land, they debated about whether to remain or sail south. Their contract with London Company officials did not give them the authority to settle in New England.

(Some historians believe that New England had been the Pilgrims' intended secret landing site from the beginning.) Regardless, they chose to stay anyway, claiming they were uncertain about the seaworthiness of their ship. Choosing to remain in New England meant they would have to govern themselves. To that end the 41 male adults onboard the *Mayflower* drew up an agreement to accept the decisions of their leaders, which they signed on November 11, 1620. Known as the Mayflower Compact, this written contract would serve as an example of self-government in English

THE MAYFLOWER COMPACT

The agreement of the Mayflower Compact was simple and straightforward, as noted in historian Mary Caroline Crawford's book, *In the Days of the Pilgrim Fathers:*

In ye name of God, Amen. We whose names are underwriten, the loyal subjects of our dread soveraigne Lord, King James, by ye grace of God, of Great Britaine, Franc, & Ireland king, defender of ye faith, &c. Having undertaken, for ye glorie of God, and advancemente of ye Christian faith, and honour of our king & countrie, a voyage to plant ye first colonie in ye Northern parts of Virginia, doe by these presents solemnly and mutually in ye presence of God, and one of another, covenant & combine ourselves together into a civil body politick, for our better ordering & preservation & furtherance of ye ends aforesaid; and by virtue hearof to enacte, constitute, and frame such just & equall lawes, ordinances, acts, constitutions, & offices, from time to time, as shall be thought most mete & convenient for ye generall good of ye Colonie, unto which we promise all due submission and obedience. In witness whereof we have hereunder subscribed our names at Cape-Codd ye II. Of November, in ye year of ye raigne of our soveragine lord, King James, of England, France, & Ireland ye eighteenth, and of Scotland ye fiftie fourth. An: Dom. 1620.

North America. Through this agreement, the men chose one of their number, John Carver, as their first governor.

During the weeks that followed, the Pilgrims explored the coast along Cape Cod Bay. They finally selected a stretch of coastline that John Smith had labeled on a 1616 map as

A map of New England made in 1635 by John Smith. He had made an earlier version in 1616 to promote colonization. Smith had asked Prince Charles—later Charles I—to replace Indian names with English ones. Plimoth was previously Accomack.

"Plimouth," so they used the name for their settlement. At Plimouth (or Plymouth), the colonists came upon a former Indian village, where land had already been cleared for farming, and a nearby freshwater stream. Situated on a hill, the site could be defended from Indians. On December 26, 1620, the Pilgrims dropped anchor at Plymouth and came ashore.

INDIAN SUPPORT AT PLYMOUTH

Having been delayed in making their voyage that fall, the Pilgrims had arrived too late to plant crops, which led to food shortages. Several colonists contracted scurvy, a disease caused by a deficiency of vitamin C. (Ironically, the Pilgrims had landed close to great numbers of cranberry bogs. Cranberries are a fruit high in vitamin C, which the Pilgrims did not know.) During their first winter at Plymouth, half of the settlers there died, just as other, earlier English colonists had at Jamestown and Roanoke.

The colony ultimately survived, thanks in part to a helpful Pawtuxet Indian named Squanto, who lived nearby. In 1605, Squanto had been taken by English fisherman in the region to England. For nearly a decade he had lived in and around London, then returned to his homeland, only to be kidnapped by another English sea captain who sold him to the Spanish as a slave. He escaped, found his way to England, and returned a second time to America in 1619, just a year before the arrival of the Pilgrims.

When the *Mayflower* arrived, Squanto was living with the Wampanoag Indians, a neighboring tribe. His Pawtuxet village had been decimated by a plague or other disease. Since he spoke English, Squanto represented the Wampanoag chief, Massasoit. Squanto taught the Pilgrims how to live off the New England landscape, giving them special instructions about raising corn and the best places to fish. Without his help, the Plymouth colony might not have survived. With

Squanto as their intermediary, the Pilgrims did not face any serious Indian problems during their first years at Plymouth. He continued to help them through their first two years, until his death by a fever in 1622.

By all accounts, the Pilgrims' first winter was dreadful, marked by disease and death. But the colonists clung to their outpost and those who survived planted crops in the spring of 1621 and saw a bountiful harvest that fall. Believing God had blessed their efforts, they decided to celebrate, and held what is now known as the first Thanksgiving.

Slowly, the Pilgrims' colony at Plymouth prospered and developed into a viable settlement with an ever-increasing population. More Separatists arrived through the colony's first 10 years, along with so-called Strangers (colonists who were not part of the religious fellowship).

THE FIRST THANKSGIVING

Writing to a friend back in England, Pilgrim Edward Winslow noted, according to historian Nathaniel Philbrick, "Our harvest being gotten in, our governor sent four men on fowling [shooting birds] that we might after a special manner rejoice together after we gathered the fruit of our labors."

The Thanksgiving celebration in the fall of 1621 lasted for three days and probably included such foods as wild fowl, deer, duck, geese, or swans, chestnuts, acorns, peas, beans, and hasty pudding, a cornmeal mush dish. Turkey could also have been included and there may have been pumpkin cooked in one form or another. Today, a typical Thanksgiving meal in America might include sweet potatoes, corn on the cob, and cranberry sauce. All of these were likely missing from the Pilgrims' feast. Indian guests, including Massasoit, brought freshly killed deer to the celebration. They may have outnumbered the Pilgrims (about 50 people) by two to one.

THE GREAT MIGRATION

During the 1620s Charles I of England continued the persecutions of the Puritans, which drove some to come to America. In 1629 a Puritan lawyer, John Winthrop, organized a group of his brethren to colonize in the New World. Plymouth's ruling body, the Council for New England, granted Winthrop's group a patent on some local land, situated between the Merrimack and Charles rivers, just north of Plymouth. The following year, they set sail in April from Yarmouth, a small port on the Isle of Wight in the south of England. Called the Great Migration, their number included more than 1,000 settlers onboard 11 ships, the largest group of colonists to leave for America to that date. They came as members of the Massachusetts Bay Company, taking their name from a local Indian tribe, the word meaning "near the great hill." They reached Massachusetts on June 12, 1630, at a place they called Salem.

Winthrop had sent an advance party over ahead of the Great Migration, to help prepare the colony site. But when the flotilla of 11 ships arrived, they found one out of four of the advance group already dead. Some were frightened, and 200 decided to return to England. Winthrop knew he would have to calm down his colonists and that would require ships to deliver much needed supplies to Salem from England. One of the ships, the *Lyon*, returned those who chose to go back to England and brought back the necessary supplies of food. In the meantime, 200 more colonists died, many having contracted scurvy. The return of the *Lyon* was a godsend: among the ship's foodstuffs was a large supply of lemons to fight scurvy.

FROM SALEM TO BOSTON

Those who remained in Salem suffered through the difficulties of the winter of 1630–31. More died, but those who survived built cabins, storehouses, and a meetinghouse for worship. The Plymouth colonists gave assistance as they could, introducing the Salem settlers to the Indian corn, clams, and seafood that they themselves had come to rely on.

When the Salem site proved inadequate for the needs of the colonists, Winthrop moved many of his people to another site to the south, which was named Charlestown. There, too, problems arose, including an inadequate water supply. So, Winthrop packed them up again to a site named Boston. This place was well chosen, and Boston soon became the main Puritan town in New England. Their population grew steadily over the following decade, and by 1640 Massachusetts Bay was home to twice as many English colonists as Virginia.

LOCAL GOVERNMENTS

As the Separatists and Puritans of New England established their colonial settlements, they formed local governments. By their views, government had the task of keeping its citizens from sin and protecting the faithful. Winthrop recognized this when he described his colony in a sermon as, in words noted by historian Allen Weinstein, "a Citty upon a Hill. The eies [eyes] of all people are uppon us." By the colony's charter, local government was to include a governor, deputy governor, and 18 assistants voted on by the company shareholders meeting in general assembly (a body called the General Court), which was to meet four times annually. Such officials were to watch over the colony's affairs, establish local laws, punish violators, hand out land to new arrivals, and otherwise maintain the order of life in Massachusetts Bay.

At first, the Puritans set up their government so that only fellow church members counted as "citizens." But as early as October 1630, when the General Court first met, several non-Puritan colonists applied for recognition as freemen, or citizens who could vote. While not all would be allowed, by May 1631, 115 freemen had taken their oaths as citizens and others were added during the years that followed. This recognition of the rights of citizenship for those outside the Puritan faith kept Massachusetts Bay from operating as a true theocracy, a combination of church and state. Church officials were never free to exercise political power over the colonists just because they were church officers. Yet, life in New England was closely monitored. Everyone in the various settlements, church member or not, was expected to attend church regularly and also to pay money to support local ministers.

THE GROWTH OF BOSTON

With each passing decade, the English colonists became more settled, lived better, and even prospered. Between 1629 and 1643, 20,000 new arrivals came to New England. With its natural harbor, Boston became a commercial beehive and additional settlements—sometimes called "hivings out," like bees establishing new hives—were established, some of them as far as 30 miles (48 kilometers) away from Boston. The world of John Smith's "New England" was one the great New World explorer might never have imagined.

5
Establishing the Thirteen Colonies

As two of the earliest English colonies established in North America, Massachusetts and Virginia soon became the most populous. They were the first in a series of 13 English colonies established along the length of the Atlantic Coast. Their creation took more than a century, with the first, Virginia (Jamestown), founded in 1607 and the last, Georgia, established in the 1730s.

NEW ENGLAND COLONIES

Some of the earliest colonial outposts did not remain separate and on their own. The colony established by the Pilgrims at Plymouth in 1621 was absorbed 70 years later into the Massachusetts Bay Colony, which had been founded by Winthrop in 1630.

Further colonies were established in New England throughout the 1600s. Rhode Island was originally populated by people who, for various reasons, left the Massachusetts Bay Colony. Anne Hutchinson and Roger Williams were both banished from Massachusetts for holding religious views that were unacceptable to the Puritan leaders. Portsmouth was settled in 1638 by a small group of people from Massachusetts Bay, including a close friend of Anne Hutchinson. Williams helped establish the settlement at Providence. He received an official land charter from King Charles I in 1644.

Other dissatisfied residents of Massachusetts moved into the fertile valley along the Connecticut River, establishing a settlement called Windsor in 1633. Three years later more colonists arrived in Connecticut, settling in Windsor, Wethersfield, and Hartford. In 1639 representatives from those three Puritan communities met and drafted the Fundamental Orders of Connecticut, an agreement that some historians recognize as the first example of a U.S. constitution based on the consent of the governed. (In some respects, it was similar to the governmental framework for Massachusetts Bay, except that it did not require membership in the Puritan faith for men to qualify as freemen, which gave them the right to vote.) Despite these important steps, the colony did not receive a charter until 1662.

RESTORATION COLONIES

Of the four New England colonies, two were established during the reign of King Charles II, the son of Charles I, who gave the land grant for Rhode Island. Charles I had been beheaded during the English Civil War of the 1640s, with a Puritan-run government replacing the monarchy for 11 years. In 1660 the monarchy was restored, which provided the name for the reign of Charles II: the Restoration. Thus, the colonies granted charters by Charles II were known as the "Restoration Colonies."

Yet another New England colony was established in New Hampshire, north of Massachusetts. An early resident was Reverend John Wheelwright, the founder of a settlement known as Exeter and the brother-in-law of Anne Hutchinson. In 1679 King Charles II granted New Hampshire colony its own charter. In all, four colonies were carved out of New England—Massachusetts (which included the area of Maine), Rhode Island, Connecticut, and New Hampshire.

ROGER WILLIAMS, FOUNDER OF RHODE ISLAND

In 1631, at age 28, Roger Williams arrived in America as a member of the Great Migration, but soon found himself on the wrong side of Puritan authorities. Williams was so strict a Puritan that, when he was offered a post as the minister of the Boston church, he refused to take it, stating that the congregation was not different, or separate, enough from the Church of England.

Within a year of his arrival, Williams decided that the colony was not legal, since the land grant did not recognize the rights of the Indians who were already living there. Unwelcome in Plymouth, he moved to another Puritan settlement, Salem. There he spoke out against the church collecting taxes to pay for itself, laws requiring colonists to attend worship services, and church leaders acting as government officials. Williams was in favor of a separation between church and state.

In the fall of 1635, the Massachusetts General Court banned Williams from the colony. In January 1636 he arrived at Narragansett Bay, in modern-day Rhode Island, and there he "purchased" land from the local Indians, establishing the settlement of Providence. Anne Hutchinson arrived in 1638. However, Williams still felt he needed a royal charter and, in 1644 received one from Parliament providing for the "Incorporation of Providence Plantations," which included Providence, Newport, Warwick, and Aquidneck, which later became Portsmouth.

ESTABLISHING THE CAROLINAS

The colony of Carolina was established under Charles II's reign and was named for him (Carolus is the Latin form of Charles). Originally a gigantic piece of property that extended from Virginia down to Spanish Florida, it had already been home to some immigrants from Virginia for years. In 1663 Charles gave the charter for Carolina to eight men, all aristocratic friends of his, and it was left to them to organize the colony and encourage settlers to move there. However, by the late 1600s the economic circumstances that had encouraged earlier migration to Virginia, Maryland, and Plymouth, no longer existed in England. With fewer incentives to move to America, fewer people did.

One of Carolina's proprietors, an aristocrat named Sir Anthony Ashley Cooper, did manage to attract colonists by offering generous land grants, including headrights of up to 150 acres (60 hectares) per person. Also, the type of government established in Carolina included religious tolerance, guarantees of English rights, such as freedom of representative assembly, as well as the institution of slavery.

Growth in the colony was slow, with only 5,000 non-Indians living in Carolina by 1675, and they were concentrated in the northern half of the colony. In the meantime, another pocket of settlement was in the southern portion of the colony, at the port of Charles Town (today's Charleston). Over the following decades, these two distinct, yet separate spheres of settlement continued, with more people arriving, including several hundred French Protestants, called Huguenots, and several Jews from Spain. By 1700 "South Carolina" alone had 6,000 non-Indian residents, half of whom were black slaves.

Prior to 1691 the northern and southern settlements of Carolina were administered as two separate colonies. Then, the attempt was made to govern them together, but North

Carolinians saw themselves as distinctly different from South Carolinians and vice versa. In 1712 Carolina was officially separated into two, distinct colonies.

NEW NETHERLAND BECOMES NEW YORK

For years during his long reign, King Charles II kept his eye on the New World, issuing new charters for more colonies. During the 1660s, New Netherland was granted a charter, even though it had already existed for 40 years as a Dutch outpost. From the early 1620s New Netherland had served the Dutch well, with the local Indians regularly trading furs for European goods. The Iroquois Indians were so eager to trade with the Dutch that they actually engaged the Huron Indians in a series of conflicts, known as the Beaver Wars, to determine who would provide the Dutch with furs. At the same time, the Dutch had pushed their European rivals, including the Swedes, out of the region centered by the Hudson River.

A decade later it was England's turn to force the Dutch out of their colonial stronghold of New Netherland. In 1664 Charles II dispatched four warships to take over the Dutch outpost. His timing was perfect. The colony's governor was a quick-tempered tyrant named Peter Stuyvesant, whose harsh rules were very unpopular with the colonists. (Stuyvesant sometimes showed his temper during council meetings in New Amsterdam, where he would bang his wooden leg against a table to make his point. He had lost that leg during a battle with the Spanish in the Caribbean.) According to historian Russell Shorto, when colonists reported his behavior and harsh ways to Dutch officials back in Holland, Stuyvesant went into a rage, shouting "People may think of appealing during my time—should any one do so, I would have him made a foot shorter, pack the pieces off to Holland and let him appeal in that way."

When the English ships showed up at the Dutch back door, the fiery Stuyvesant was ready to defend his place and his colony. Unfortunately for him, almost no one else was ready to support him. Regardless of the will of the people or of Stuyvesant, defending the colonists against the English warships was impossible. The colony did not have much gunpowder on hand or even bullets with which to defend themselves. On September 8, 1664, the Dutch gave up New Netherland to the English. The colony became the property of the king's brother, James, the Duke of York, and the name of New Netherland was forever changed to New York.

LIFE IN NEW YORK

Without ever leaving England, the Duke of York acquired the colony of New Netherland through the forced surrender of the Dutch colony to English warships. But even as the English gained control of another European power's North American outpost, little changed for the 40-year-old colony. Hardly anyone left the colony as rule shifted to England, and Dutch continued to be spoken for many years.

Those colonists living in New Netherland were not just of Dutch ancestry, but represented a multicultural population where at least 18 languages were spoken. At the time, the settlement of New Amsterdam was the second largest town along the Atlantic seaboard, with Boston as the most populous. Alongside the Dutch were Swedes, Finns, English, Indians, and even a dozen or so Jews from Brazil. (During those years, New Amsterdam was the only Atlantic seaboard colony to allow Jews to live there.) In addition, the former Dutch town boasted a good number of black residents, numerous enough to account for one out of every five.

When the English took control, the lives of many residents improved, beginning with the granting of the rights of Englishmen to everyone by 1674. Within another 10 years

THE SURRENDER OF NEW AMSTERDAM

In September 1664, British ships entered Gravesend Bay in what is today Brooklyn and quickly overcame the Dutch colony. On September 8, the Dutch West India Company's colors were struck and Dutch troops started the journey home to the Netherlands. Thomas Willett, at one time captain of the Plymouth colony, became the first mayor of New York.

The document of September 8, 1664, signed by Peter Stuyvesant, surrendering the Dutch colony to the English.

the Duke of York also allowed his colonists to establish an elected assembly.

THE COLONY OF NEW JERSEY

Some residents of New Netherland never experienced life under the proprietorship of the Duke of York. In 1664 James chose to divide his colony and hand off the lands that today comprise New Jersey to some friends of his, Sir George Carteret and Lord John Berkeley. (These two had already been proprietors of an Atlantic seaboard colony, as they had been two of the eight who established Carolina.) The colony became known as New Jersey.

While the Duke of York did not take anything like a hands-on approach with New York, Berkeley and Carteret did with New Jersey. In February 1665 they announced a policy called the Concessions and Agreements Act, designed to attract colonists. The act promised would-be residents that a legislative assembly would be created, that free trade would be available to all who wanted to participate, and there would be religious toleration to any Protestant group (Catholics were not included). In what was becoming the pattern for colonial government in North America, the pair of proprietors also put in place a governor and an advisory council. When the general assembly was formed, it held the power to tax New Jersey residents.

The proprietors also handed out generous land grants to new arrivals. While Carteret and Berkeley were allowed to keep as personal property one out of every seven acres (2.8 hectares) of New Jersey land, they also made available 150 acres (60 ha) for every immigrating family head, plus an additional 150 acres (60 ha) for every servant, to be held by his or her master. But each servant was given 75 acres (30 ha) of land once he or she had lived in the colony for at least four years.

Even as Berkeley and Carteret established New Jersey in 1665, a cousin of Carteret's, Philip, sailed to America to become New Jersey's first lieutenant governor. One of his first headaches after arriving was to take up the responsibility of trying to sort all the confusing and sometimes overlapping land claims that predated the takeover of New Netherland by the English. Some of those claims went back decades. In 1674 Lord Berkeley sold off his interest in West Jersey to a pair of Quaker men, with one of them selling his newly acquired lands to a group of Quakers. (Carteret kept possession and control of East Jersey for himself.) A member of that group was a Quaker named William Penn, who would later establish the colony of Pennsylvania.

PENN'S EARLY LIFE

William Penn was the son of Sir William Penn, the lord admiral of King Charles II. As a young aristocrat, Penn attended first Oxford, then Cambridge University, and then joined the royal diplomatic corps. His road to success had been paved with privilege. But Penn soon altered his life course forever when he converted and became a member of the Society of Friends, known as the Quakers. Becoming a Quaker was a monumental decision for Penn. Already prepared to serve in the king's military, he had to give up a potential officer's rank, for the Quakers were pacifists and did not participate in war. Penn was attracted by the Christian simplicity of the Quakers and their belief that all people are created equal. Since the Quakers were persecuted in England at that time, Penn sometimes found himself arrested for his faith, despite his father's friendship with the king.

About 10 years after Penn's conversion to the Society of Friends, his father died. Years earlier, King Charles II had borrowed heavily from the wealthy, elder Penn, and the debt then transferred to Penn's son, William. When the king tried to repay his debt, the younger Penn asked for the payment to be made in American land. After all, he was already one of the proprietors of the colony of New Jersey, so he saw the opportunity to add to his existing holdings in the New World. The king granted Penn a charter for a colony that

A copy of folk artist Edward Hick's 1847 painting of William Penn's treaty with the Indians of 1681 to establish the colony of Pennsylvania. Penn also made treaties with Swedish, Dutch, Finnish, and English settlers who had previously inhabited the area.

extended from the Delaware River five degrees longitude west and from the 40th degree to the 43rd degree of north latitude. King Charles II had no idea just how generous he had been to William Penn. In total the area of the land grant was more than 45,000 square miles (120,000 square kilometers)—almost equivalent to that of England! Still, Penn wanted more and even got an agreement from Charles to add additional land lying west of Delaware Bay to his already enormous properties. William Penn the Younger had certainly made a great land deal.

"PENN'S SYLVANIA"

It was Charles II who named this new colony as Pennsylvania, or Penn's Sylvania, meaning "Penn's Woods." Penn would have preferred another name, as Quakers were not much for pretense and showing off. Besides, other English colonies had been already named for monarchs and royalty—Virginia, Carolina, Maryland, New York. Still, Charles would not hear of anything else, informing young Penn that he was naming the colony not after him, but after his father.

William Penn wasted almost no time at all before calling for colonists to sail to America and take residence in his colony. And of all the colonial proprietors, Penn stands as one of the best examples of how to establish a colony right and fairly. Although he wanted his colony to serve as a haven for fellow Quakers, he also allowed for complete religious tolerance of all Christian groups. He established a political structure that he called the Frame of Government. This included himself, the proprietor, as the colony's governor, plus a deputy governor and a council of assistants, whose members were elected by the colony's freeholders, all of whom were landowners. (It was the assembly that created the Great Law in 1682, which established religious freedom in Pennsylvania.)

A House in the New Colonies

The new colonists built houses following the style of their original countries. The English settlers built with wood from the rich forests. The drawing shows a house in Massachusetts from the 1670s. The houses had tall central chimneys and a strong timber frame resting on stone foundations.

1. Brick chimney
2. Shingle roof
3. Wood frame
4. Glass windows
5. Stone foundations

6. Parlor
7. Cooking Fire
8. Kitchen
9. Wooden furniture
10. Bedroom

A HANDS-ON APPROACH

Taking a step that was rare among proprietors, Penn also met early on with local Indians, such as the Delaware, and "purchased" the land from them. He also tried to monitor the trade that took place between the Indians and white traders to make certain the American Indians were not cheated. Penn took such a hands-on approach with his colony, he even laid out the streets for his new colonial city, Philadelphia, a name taken from the Bible, which meant "brotherly love." The streets were placed in a checkerboard pattern of intersecting lanes, along with open, public green spaces, such as commons and parks. Penn named several of his streets according to the various trees that were located close by, such as Chestnut, Pine, and Walnut. As often as he could, Penn kept trees standing so his city would be more attractive.

Philadelphia proved a popular destination for colonists. Between 1682 and 1689 more than four dozen merchants and shopkeepers set up business in the new Pennsylvania community. Another three dozen or so came in by 1700. By then Philadelphia was home to 10,000 people. Penn's colony attracted people from England, Ireland, Scotland, Sweden, Finland, and Holland, as well as thousands from various German states.

PROBLEMS FOR PENN

Many things went well for Penn in his establishment of his community. However, he spent money too quickly, eventually going through nearly all of his father's fortune. Then, he ran into trouble with his colony. He chose to reduce the number of council members from 72 to 18, with his intent being to make the colony run more efficiently. The move proved unpopular. Some people believed he was filling council seats with his friends. He also upset some by his tendency to micromanage the colony, busying himself with all sorts of small details. After only two years in his colony, Penn felt the need to leave for England. Fifteen years would pass before he ever returned to Pennsylvania.

When he did sail back to America in 1699, with plans to take back direct control of his colony, he found himself on the outside looking in. The assembly did not want to give up control, and Penn was soon caught up in a political struggle. In 1701 he received word that the Crown was going to take over all proprietary colonies, such as Pennsylvania. He went back to England to fight for his proprietorship, but failed. He died in 1718, having never been back to Pennsylvania again.

THE SWEDES, DUTCH, AND DELAWARE

Of all the original 13 English colonies scattered along the Atlantic seaboard, the one that had the most difficult and complicated start was the smallest, Delaware. During its early colonial history, it was actually part of two different colonies before managing to form itself into only one. For hundreds

THE MARGRAVATE OF AZILIA

In 1717 the lands lying between Spanish-held Florida and South Carolina were granted to Sir Robert Montgomery as proprietor. Montgomery had plans to establish his New World realm as a military colony, with himself as military ruler or margrave, in order to keep Spain from encroaching further north. But his plans to establish the so-called Margravate of Azilia fizzled out, and Montgomery lost his proprietorship for not planting a colony. Azilia became part of the Carolina colony until 1729, when Carolina split in two, and then its future as a single colony was revived when an Englishman called James Edward Oglethorpe showed an interest in the region.

of years prior to the arrival of the English, Delaware had been home to the Leni-Lenape Indians, who lived in small villages where they hunted, farmed, and fished. Once Europeans arrived in their region, the Leni-Lenape dropped in significant numbers due to exposure to new diseases, leading the tribe to move to Canada.

The Dutch were among the first Europeans to reach the shores of modern-day Delaware, and the Leni-Lenape gave them permission to hunt whales off the Delaware coast. In 1638 the Swedes arrived and built a trading post on the Delaware River, naming it Fort Christina after their queen. Peter Minuit, who had formerly served as governor of New Netherland, was the Swedes' leader. From their outpost, the Swedes traded for furs from the Indians. They introduced a new type of house to America—the log cabin—and also brought their religion, Lutheranism. They also raised fields of rye and barley, which they used to brew beer. Despite these factors, the Swedish colony did not grow much. After 10 years of colonizing, Fort Christina and the surrounding Swedish lands were home to no more than 200 persons.

With such few numbers, the Swedish colony was an easy target for others, including the Dutch who took over in 1655. However, when the English took over New Netherland less than 10 years later, the Swedes came under new control. By 1682 the underpopulated colony was part of Penn's land grant. In the 1690s the people settled around the Delaware petitioned the proprietor for permission to separate out from Pennsylvania. Penn agreed, and in 1704 Delaware came into its own as a colony, with Penn remaining only technically as proprietor. By this time, the residents of Delaware were busy growing tobacco as their cash crop, bringing slaves into the region. Additional towns developed, and Fort Christina eventually became the community of Wilmington, today the largest city in Delaware.

GEORGIA: REFORMER COLONY

Another generation passed before the last of the 13 colonies was established. The colony of Georgia was founded by James Edward Oglethorpe, an Oxford graduate and member of Parliament, who was involved in various social reform efforts. In particular he believed that the system of debtors' prison—imprisoning people who owed money until their debts were paid—was inhumane and to the disadvantage of the poor. Oglethorpe approached King George II about the lands known at that time as Azilia, suggesting that debtors could be moved there to build the colony and provide military service against possible menace by the Spanish in Florida. The Crown agreed.

In 1732 Parliament chartered the colony, appointing Oglethorpe as its governor. Oglethorpe sailed along with 120 would-be colonists to Charleston, South Carolina. They remained there through the winter of 1732–1733, then moved south to search out a possible settlement site. Oglethorpe selected a location on some hills overlooking the Savannah River, where he, much like William Penn had done in Philadelphia, paced off the streets and the sites for housing lots and commons. Oglethorpe named his colony Georgia, after the king.

As Oglethorpe set up his colony, he had specific ideas about what he would and would not allow. He did not like slavery, so the institution was banned. He also barred rum and declared the local Indians must be treated humanely and fairly. The colony was otherwise open to anyone, and early immigrants included German Lutherans, Jews from Austria and Portugal, Scottish highlanders, and others. By the end of 10 years as a colony, Georgia was home to 1,000 non-Indian settlers. Still, growth was slow.

In 1753 Georgia was taken over as a royal colony. The restrictions on rum and slavery were lifted and treatment of the Indians worsened. By this time, Oglethorpe was no longer in control of his reform-minded colony. It was run by a British governor appointed by George II.

THE THIRTEEN COLONIES

During the 1600s the competition for New World colonies had hit its stride. Ultimately, the French and English dominated North America. The French placed themselves in the St. Lawrence River Valley, concentrating their efforts in the extensive fur trade, their outposts remaining small, scattered, and undermanned. By 1700 New France (modern-day Canada) was home to few French residents, but the trade they supported was lucrative, causing French monarchs to provide ongoing, hands-on support.

The English monarchy was less directly involved in the establishment of the English colonies along the Atlantic Coast. Typically, colonial organizers received permission, or charters, from specific kings and queens, sometimes raising money for their ventures through the selling of stock in a joint-stock company, such as the London (or Virginia) Company that financed Jamestown. Others, such as the Calverts, William Penn, and the Duke of York, were appointed as proprietors and invested their own capital in their royally chartered American properties. This meant that those Englishmen who founded colonies in America took great risks, having little direct support from the Crown, while the French and Spanish operated their colonies through royal bureaucracies whose kings and queens held true stake in the future of their national extensions of power.

With little pressure from the Crown on how to organize their colonies, English colonial organizers began to allow common English government systems, including elected assemblies, councils, and governors. The English colonies also enjoyed the advantage of great latitude in determining

THE THIRTEEN COLONIES

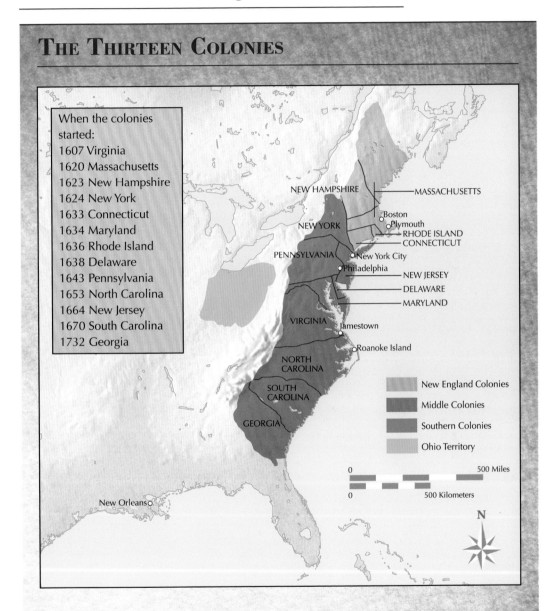

When the colonies started:
1607 Virginia
1620 Massachusetts
1623 New Hampshire
1624 New York
1633 Connecticut
1634 Maryland
1636 Rhode Island
1638 Delaware
1643 Pennsylvania
1653 North Carolina
1664 New Jersey
1670 South Carolina
1732 Georgia

NEW HAMPSHIRE — MASSACHUSETTS
Boston
NEW YORK — Plymouth
RHODE ISLAND
CONNECTICUT
PENNSYLVANIA — New York City
Philadelphia — NEW JERSEY
— DELAWARE
— MARYLAND
VIRGINIA — Jamestown
Roanoke Island
NORTH CAROLINA
SOUTH CAROLINA
GEORGIA
New Orleans

New England Colonies
Middle Colonies
Southern Colonies
Ohio Territory

0   500 Miles
0   500 Kilometers

N

A map of the 13 English colonies in 1733. They were divided into three regions. At this time, Maine was part of Massachusetts. These colonies became the first United States of America. Following the French and Indian War of 1755–63, the colonies expanded westward toward the Great Lakes in the north and the Appalachian Mountains in the west.

how their local economies operated, what industries were established, and how their societies functioned. The result was a collection of colonies that were unique and independent—an English presence that relied on individualism, freedom of thought and religion, and groups of men and women who made their way through the world as they saw fit.

6
The Colonies Mature

As the colonial era progressed, the extreme trials faced by early settlers decreased, but the societies became more complex. The result was a collection of colonies connected by common English culture, with each functioning somewhat on its own. Life in Massachusetts was very different than that in Georgia, for example. Historians divide the 13 colonies into three regions: New England, the Middle Colonies, and the South. Each region had its unique characteristics, lifestyles, and social systems.

NEW ENGLAND'S TOWN SYSTEM

New England was one of the earlier English colonial worlds to develop, starting with the landing of the Pilgrims in 1620. (Even prior to that date, English fisherman had made temporary fishing colonies in the region.) From the beginning, the social pattern of New England was determined by the way land was distributed. To encourage town settlement and growth, people were put in groups close to one another, with a group holding land in common, or communally. This "town system," was first used in the Massachusetts Bay Colony and spread from there.

Typically, a group of newly arrived families approached the General Court for permission to organize a town. The Court examined the group's members to make certain they were all Puritans. Then they would assign a town site. The group transplanted itself to this piece of property and appointed town officials called proprietors. In many cases, these early town grants included a block of land measuring 6 miles (nearly 10 kilometers) square.

Together, the new residents decided on the sites for the meetinghouse, houses, village green, and farmland. The meetinghouse was both a church and a place where the residents gathered to talk about local politics and make decisions about their community. During town meetings, the residents also selected their representatives to the General

THE PURITAN WAY OF LIFE

Because their religion was so important to them as a daily reminder of how to lead honest, sober lives, while remaining keenly aware of God's will for everyone, the Puritans are often remembered for little else today. The word "puritanical" is often used as a negative reference for someone who is prudish, narrow-minded, overly strict when disciplining, and self-righteous.

However, the Puritans should not be thought of so simply. They were not ignorant people opposed to everything fun. Enjoying the company they shared with their fellow believers could bring them joy.

Unlike the stereotype, Puritans did not always wear drab, black and white clothing. They enjoyed color, and their clothes often featured deep shades of orange, red, blue, yellow,

Court in Boston—yet another example of early democracy in colonial America.

A 1647 law in Massachusetts required all Puritan towns of 50 families or more to build a school for the local children. If a town had 100 families, it must also open a grammar school for the boys, to prepare them in their Latin studies so they might go on to college and train as Puritan ministers. Such supports of education meant that colonial New England boasted the highest literacy rate of any of the English colonies, a rate that was even greater than that found in many European countries.

THE PURITAN RELIGION

Nothing had motivated the Pilgrims to settle in New England more than had their religion. Persecuted in England, they had arrived in America in 1620 ready to establish their faith traditions in the New World and worship God as they pleased. In the early decades, the Puritans established their local

purple, and brown—hues they called the "sadd colours." But they were opposed to wearing flashy, gaudy, or elaborate clothing that made someone stand out as if he or she wanted to be noticed.

Their religion, nevertheless, sometimes caused the Puritans to become overly pious and judgmental. They believed their ideas about religion were true and that differing ideas might constitute false teaching. Puritans thought that strict morality played an important role in helping keep Christians pure and unspotted from the world around them. As a result, the Puritans created many rules about how to act on a day-to-day basis.

Puritan worship services were typically simple, involving congregational singing, prayer, communion, and long sermons. It was typical for Puritan ministers to present sermons that ran one or two hours long, sometimes longer.

government and authority as an extension of their religion, with their religious leaders serving as state officials. The colonies of Massachusetts, Connecticut, New Hampshire, and Rhode Island were all established as communities of believers, most of whom were not interested in sharing their colonies with, or giving the same religious freedoms to, people who believed differently from them.

Decades passed before the Puritans of New England gave up some of their religious bigotry and accepted other religious groups. Those earlier decades included regular persecutions of the Quakers and Baptists who found their way into one New England colony or another.

In 1689 the English Parliament passed the Toleration Act, which stated that no colonial government had the right to determine what religion was acceptable, that all church beliefs had to be voluntary, and that no one could be forced to support one group over another. No longer could New England require its citizens to practice their faith within the Puritan religion.

SHRINKING CONGREGATIONS

At the same time, the Puritans were having trouble within their own ranks. With each passing year, Puritan congregations declined in numbers. Puritan ministers referred to this phenomenon as "declension." Each new generation of the faithful attended Puritan worship services less often, especially after attendance was no longer required by law. One problem was that the earliest Puritans had become members of the faith by choice, whereas forced enrollment had required people to participate without a personal conversion experience. In 1662 the Puritans developed a new theology practice called the Halfway Covenant, which allowed church members, including some of the Puritans' own unconverted children, to become "halfway" members. This meant they were baptized, an act considered essential for salvation and church membership, but denied communion.

By 1700 much of the fervor of the Pilgrims and other founding Puritans seemed lost in an earlier time. One group of Puritans, who became known as Congregationalists, were not prepared to watch their faith dwindle. In 1729 a new minister took the pulpit of the Congregationalist church in Northampton, Massachusetts. His name was Jonathan Edwards, and he was disappointed at how lukewarm many

PURITANS AND WITCHCRAFT

One specific Puritan theology that was put to the test during the late 1600s was a belief in witchcraft. The Puritans believed Satan had the power to possess people and cause them to participate in evil activities of all sorts. (In Europe, the practice was taken so seriously that thousands of people, mostly women, were convicted as witches and executed.)

Between 1630 and 1700, approximately 150 people were accused of witchcraft in New England, of whom about 40 were executed, usually by hanging. There were never any witch burnings in the English colonies at any time.

The most notorious witchcraft trials in America took place during the 1690s in the New England settlement of Salem. A group of Puritan girls became obsessed with Satanic stories of possession and began accusing others of being witches. Fear gripped Salem. Although the girls made hundreds of accusations, 50 people went to trial and admitted their guilt, just to avoid execution. But another 20 maintained their innocence. They were found guilty and sentenced to death. (The court also found two dogs guilty.) The 19 convicted women were hanged. The one "warlock" was laid on the ground with a door on top of him, upon which rocks were piled up until he was crushed to death.

When the girls were adults, several admitted they had lied, and that the Salem witchcraft trials had resulted in the deaths of innocent victims.

George Whitefield came to America in 1738 and was made parish priest in Savannah, Georgia. He traveled widely through the colonies, preaching every day for months on end. He became friends with Benjamin Franklin, who published his works.

Puritans had become and how much more liberal the Congregationalist faith was compared to that of their forefathers. Edwards decided something had to be done.

THE GREAT AWAKENING

Jonathan Edwards and an English evangelist named George Whitefield called for a new era of religious revivalism. The result was called the Great Awakening, which began during the 1730s and peaked in the late 1740s. In their sermons, Whitefield and Edwards, as well as other ministers of like mind, called for fuller, more emotional conversion experiences. Primarily these preachers spoke outdoors at large gatherings, offering salvation to anyone who was prepared to follow Jesus. In part, the Great Awakening was a call for a revived brand of Christianity, one that was grounded in personal faith and religious fervor. The movement was highly effective, as well as democratic. Sermons appealed to every class and race, so that blacks and the colonial underclass of poor people found a new avenue of faith. A new Puritanism, one with more heart and soul, was the result.

NEW ENGLAND DEVELOPS

Most of the expansion of the New England colonies took place gradually during the 1600s and early 1700s. By mid-eighteenth century there was little land that had not yet been assigned. At the same time, the Indian populations in New England had dropped.

When Plymouth was founded in 1620–1621, and for several decades to follow, there had been little violence between the indigenous groups in the region and the English settlers. Any skirmishes were local and shortlived. Some Indian nations had established early trade connections and occasionally used English colonists as allies against their traditional Indian enemies. This meant that, through a repeated pattern of alliances and loyalties, Indians sometimes brought about the deaths of other Indians.

Over time, problems developed between American Indians and the Europeans who encroached upon their lands. At the heart of these conflicts were the differences in the way in which each group viewed the land. The English believed that an individual could hold the property rights to a piece of land and exert control over its uses. Private property ownership was a foreign concept to many American Indians, who saw land as something to be used communally, meaning held by the group, not by a single person. Given these different views, it is not surprising that the English and the Indians might have different interpretations and opinions about a given treaty.

If an Indian leader signed a treaty over land, he probably thought he was granting permission to share the land with his white neighbors. The English, on the other hand, thought they were purchasing the land and that the Indians were giving up all rights to it. With these two divergent views competing with one another, confusion and conflict were inevitable.

EARLY INDIAN CONFLICTS

Early conflicts between whites and American Indians in New England were more about Indians using the European arrivals as allies. In 1623, only a couple of years after the landing of the *Mayflower*, the Wampanoag chief, Massasoit, talked the Pilgrims into banding with them and attacking their traditional Indian enemies. The Pilgrims' military leader, Miles Standish, returned from such an assault with the head of the enemy leader on a pike, which he displayed outside the Pilgrims' settlement. This proved even too gruesome to the Wampanoags, who began referring to the local English as the *wotowquenange,* which translates as "cutthroats."

On Good Friday in 1622, Powhatan Indians attacked the Virginia colony of Jamestown and killed some 340 people, one quarter of the population. The Powhatan then burned the colonists' homes and crops.

In 1636, New England colonists fell into a conflict with the local Pequot tribe, following the death of a Boston-based trader, which the colonials blamed on the Indians. (In fact, the Pequot had nothing to do with his death.) When the conflict broke out, another tribe, the Narraganset, allied with the colonials against the Pequot, taking advantage of the situation. The militias of Plymouth and Massachusetts Bay colonies joined together to fight the Pequot. The resulting year-long Pequot War included the massacre of men, women, and children in the Pequot's main village. Some Pequot victims were turned into slaves.

KING PHILIP'S WAR

In 1675 a new Indian war broke out in New England, and this time the English fought the Wampanoag, rather than have them as allies. At issue was the refusal of the Wampanoag to accept English authority over them and their lands. The Wampanoag' leader was Metacom, also known as King Philip. Although his people had enjoyed a half-century of peace with the English, soon violence erupted between the two groups, and bloodshed spread up and down the New England frontier. The war dragged on for a year, with Metacom and his warriors burning colonial houses, barns, and corncribs, and slaughtering English people in their path. The Indians attacked the Plymouth village of Swansea, then allied themselves to other Indian tribes, launching a campaign along the western Massachusetts backcountry. The settlement of Pocumtuck was set on fire. As the violence spread and increased, Englishmen struck back hard.

Throughout those months of war, the Indian nations in New England were almost completely wiped out. Metacom was shot and killed by an Indian guide who was leading a party of Englishmen. By the time the war ended, King Philip's War had brought about the deaths of one out of every 16 whites in New England, as well as countless Indians. Some experts believe that, by the war's end, half of the Indians who had been living in New England before the war had either been killed or had completely fled the region.

TOWN GROWTH IN NEW ENGLAND

By the 1700s New England life had matured in many ways. The old connections between church and state had begun to decline, even as the original settlement pattern, the old town system, blossomed. In some cases, New England towns hit their highest populations during the 1600s, then declined in population by the early 1700s. Still others continued to see steady growth. These larger towns and cities—especially those located along the seacoast—were an important part of the economy of New England.

Such old Puritan communities as Boston and Salem in Massachusetts and Newport, Rhode Island, had, by the mid-eighteenth century, developed economies that included merchandising, banking, shipbuilding, and shipping. The latter had always been an important aspect of New England life. As early as the 1660s, New England trading vessels were plying the waters of the Caribbean. By the 1700s the West Indies served as the destination for half of all New England-exported goods. Ships carried such items as dried fish, stowed away in barrels; cattle and other livestock; lumber and wood products; and whale products, including whale oil and spermaceti (a waxy substance extracted from the head of the whale, which colonials used to make high quality, almost smokeless candles).

LIFE IN THE MIDDLE COLONIES

By the beginning of the 1700s the Middle Colonies—New York, Pennsylvania, New Jersey, and Delaware—were home to some of the most significant population diversity, as well as the two largest cities in the colonies, and the continent's most advanced and progressive economies. Trade, shipping, and merchandising were among the dominant elements of the Middle Colonies' economies.

Although the Middle Colonies were typically founded later, growth in the region was dramatic. In 1700, New York's population had reached just under 20,000 residents. Sixty years later, New York was home to 117,000—nearly six times as many people. The colony of Pennsylvania grew from 18,000 to 180,000 during those same decades. New Jersey's population increased nearly sevenfold, from 14,000 to 93,000, while tiny Delaware expanded from 2,500 to 33,000—the largest rate of growth of all four Middle Colonies. Not only did existing towns grow but, between 1740 and 1770, more than 50 new communities were founded in the Middle Colonies.

BACON'S REBELLION

During the months of King Philip's War in New England in 1675–1676, another Indian-related conflict erupted to the south. However, this conflict soon became more about a rebellion by whites.

In January 1676 the Virginia frontier experienced several Indian raids, resulting in the deaths of dozens of colonists. The Tidewater planters and backwoods residents around Jamestown called on the governor, Sir William Berkeley, to protect them, but he was slow to raise a force. The colonists took events in their own hands and went on counter raids of their own. A full-scale Indian war looked unavoidable.

One of the ringleaders was 28-year-old Nathaniel Bacon, a well-bred Englishman who was actually Berkeley's cousin by marriage, and who had recently arrived in Virginia to farm a 1,000-acre (400-hectare) estate up the James River. When Bacon led a group of planters against

New York and Philadelphia were already becoming crowded and congested. The streets were packed with carts and wagons, and anyone crossing a street had to watch out for horse-drawn traffic, including runaway teams and, in winter, horse sleighs. The truckers and deliverymen of the colonial era—the carters or cartmen—wove through traffic, sometimes racing other cartmen to a shop or a store to sell their wares. Serious accidents and deaths were common and plentiful on these urban highways.

Ethnic Diversity

Those who had migrated to the Middle Colonies made up a colorful stew of multiculturalism. Just looking at New York City shows a diverse set of neighborhoods. Over in the city's Flatbush district were the Dutch. French Protestants (Huguenots) lived in New Rochelle. The Flemish made their

the Indians, Governor Berkeley quickly had him arrested.

It was then that the backcountry folk identified Bacon as a hero—someone who took the situation in hand even as the governor dawdled. Under pressure, Berkeley released Bacon on condition he stopped his campaigns. In June Bacon returned to Jamestown with 500 followers, requesting permission to fight the Indians again. Hesitantly, Berkeley agreed, but then took back his order, and called for Bacon's arrest. Bacon and his supporters marched on Jamestown and burned down the Virginia capital.

Bacon's Rebellion did not last much longer, for Bacon died of dysentery in July, his body covered with lice. And Bacon was hardly a heroic figure. He and his men had killed wantonly, not even attacking those Indians who had carried out the attacks they were supposedly avenging. But Bacon had called for a revolt against Virginia's governor and even spoke about independence from English authority a century before the American Revolution.

This modern reenactment at the Governor's Palace in Williamsburg, Virginia shows us what life was like in the Southern colonies.

homes in Bergen County, while the Scots settled in Perth Amboy. There were black slaves in New York, living along the lower Hudson Valley, accounting for 15 percent of the local residents.

The Middle Colonies had provided refuge for a diverse collection of religious believers, including Catholics, Quakers, Congregationalists (the descendents of the Puritans), Baptists, Mennonites, and Jews. Each was able to practice his or her religious convictions without fear of persecution. The vast majority of the Germans who migrated to these colonies were Lutherans or Calvinists.

RELIGIOUS GROUPS

Although the vast number of colonists were from England or Scotland, there were plenty of other groups, both ethnic and religious. Irish and Italian Catholics and a diversity of Jews were scattered through many of the colonies, with concentrations in Rhode Island and New York. French Protestants called Huguenots found their way to the colonies during the latter decades of the 1600s, settling by the hundreds in Massachusetts, Rhode Island, New York, Pennsylvania, Virginia, and the Carolinas.

Welsh Baptists and Quakers often made their homes in the middle colonies and the backcountry of the southern colonies. Swiss Mennonites arrived in Lancaster County, Pennsylvania, in 1710, where their religious descendents, the Amish, still make their homes and follow their traditions. Pietist groups from Germany, including the Moravians, came to America, where several settled in Georgia.

THE SOUTHERN COLONIES

With the colonial South stretching from the upper reaches of Chesapeake Bay to the northern border of Spanish Florida, the region covered a great deal of territory. The five colonies of the South—Maryland, Virginia, North Carolina, South Carolina, and Georgia—could easily be considered as two sub-regions: The Chesapeake or Tidewater South and the Lower South. The older of the two was the Tidewater, which comprised Virginia and Maryland. The Lower South was the Carolinas and Georgia. The southern colonies were not even settled in the same century; Georgia was founded some 125 years after Jamestown, Virginia.

The racial makeup of the southern colonies provides a different profile than some of the other colonial regions. Three distinct racial groups represented the greater number of people living in the South. The whites, almost all of them of European descent, included English, Germans, Austrians, Scots, Irish, Welsh, and French. The second group in number were blacks, the vast majority of whom were slaves living in bondage and working on white-owned farms and planta-

RELIGION IN THE SOUTH

While New Englanders supported Puritanism and, later, Congregationalism as their religious preference, English officials in the Tidewater region tended to support the Church of England—the same religious body from which the Puritans escaped. At times, Virginia allowed no other church than the Anglican faith. Residents were required to attend worship services of the Church of England and were required to pay taxes in support of the Anglican church.

tions. Black slaves comprised 40 percent of the South's population by the mid-eighteenth century. The third group was the region's original inhabitants, the Indians. Their ancestors had greeted the first European arrivals in the late 1500s. Most had been pushed or encouraged to move away from the Atlantic Coast into the interior, where they sometimes established and maintained trade connections with whites.

During the 1600s the settlements established in the South were located along the Atlantic Coast. By 1700 people had not only filled out the coastal landscape, but also moved inland, often following the many rivers that flowed from the east side of the Appalachian Mountains to the coast. This inland region, lying between the mountains and the coast, includes the great valleys that constitute the Piedmont, a country of rich farmland. This encouraged western movement since most colonials practiced agriculture of some sort. In fact, the South was extremely rural during the colonial period, with few cities.

PLANTATIONS AND FARMS

With nearly everyone farming, the pattern of settlement was that people scattered up and down the various rivers that had carried them inland. The dominant crops raised were tobacco, rice, and indigo. As the eighteenth century advanced, the most significant social and economic institution of the South was the plantation, a large farm that relied on slave labor for the field work. By 1750 a typical southern plantation was dominated by a mansion, sometimes occupying high ground that overlooked the owner's fields, and known to the slaves as the "big house." Outbuildings might include a smokehouse, summer kitchen, barns, stables, corncribs, and drying sheds, where tobacco leaves were hung from the rafters to cure. The slaves usually lived in small, wooden cabins with dirt floors. These slave quarters were not built

A Southern Slave Plantation 1770

A plantation house and the farm and slave
   buildings from around 1770. The grand house
   was occupied by the owner and his family.
   The slaves lived in the huts around the
   farm buildings. The slaves worked in the
   fields behind the slave houses.

1. Plantation house
2. Owner's backyard
3. House slaves' house
4. Kitchen garden
5. Plantation house kitchen
6. Planter's carriage
7. Barns
8. Farmyard
9. Slaves' houses
10. Farm fields

for comfort, and were often hot in summer and very cold in winter. Many housed more than one family.

While wealthy plantation owners dominated southern life, significant numbers of white southerners were poor farmers who owned smaller plots of land and scratched out a living raising crops of tobacco. Tobacco provided the best profits during the colonial period. Such small-scale farmers might own a slave or two, but they were usually found in the fields working alongside their slaves. These farmers tended to move often. With little fertilizer in use, the tobacco fields were quickly sapped of nutrients, so the soil was worn out after five to seven years.

SLAVERY IN THE COLONIES

The 13 colonies were founded by Englishmen and women who had almost all come voluntarily, seeking new opportunities in the New World. However, one group of colonists did not come to America by choice. They were Africans who were forcibly removed from their tribal worlds, captured and bought, then transported to the New World on slave ships. Most were shipped to North America via the West Indies.

These slaves eventually provided a workforce, even if the numbers of slaves delivered to North America was only 5 percent of the total number of slaves brought to the Western Hemisphere. This reliance on black slaves did not take place overnight nor was it common to all the colonies. Jamestown saw its first blacks dropped off by a Dutch slaver in 1619; through the following half-century or longer, few additional Africans were landed in the colonies.

The colonies did not generally need black labor during the 1600s. White indentured servants were available in large numbers, and they cost half as much as a slave to import. Indentured servants were those who could not pay their own ship passage to America. Instead, someone else paid,

An advertisement for a slave auction published in the June 23, 1768, issue of the *New York Journal, or General Advertiser*. Newspapers of the time regularly included ads offering captured slaves for sale and financial rewards for finding and returning runaway slaves to their owners.

and the new immigrant, usually in his or her late teens or early twenties, worked off the debt over a period of typically seven years.

After 1700, better economic conditions in England led to a decline in the availability of indentured servants and a greater reliance on black slave labor. Eighty thousand Africans were imported to Virginia and Maryland alone between 1700 and 1770. The Lower South was home to approximately 90,000 slaves.

Keeping the Labor Force Alive

While slavery was a harsh institution by its very existence, the slavery practiced in the British colonies of North America was somewhat different from slave systems found elsewhere in the Western Hemisphere. Many of the slaves purchased in the Caribbean or in South America were used on sugar plantations. The labor was so strenuous that many slaves died after four or five years, but sugar plantations made so much money that owners could afford to replace their slaves in a short turnaround time.

In North America, no such lucrative crop was produced. Tobacco profits might be good, but they were no match for sugar. Slave owners could not "afford" to work their slaves to death in just a few years. To be profitable, the slave had to provide many more years of work. The result was that slave owners in the 13 colonies treated their slaves so that they would live longer. With more slaves surviving longer in North America, slaves were able to have children. This phenomenon, called natural increase, did not take place in any other slave region of the Western Hemisphere. By the time of the American Revolution (the 1770s and 1780s) most slaves in the colonies were not directly from Africa, but had been born in America.

7

The Fight for the Ohio Country

By the 1750s, 13 separate, yet very English, colonies had been established. Some had been around for nearly 150 years. However, colonizing in other parts of the Americas had been going on for more than 250 years, as several key European powers had carved out a presence in the New World, including the French in Canada and the Caribbean, the English also in the Caribbean, the Spanish in Central and South America, and the Portuguese in Brazil. While some colonies remained unrivaled in their regional power, the colonies of one power were sometimes so close to the colonies of another European power that conflict developed over where one colony began and the other ended. Add the fact that these and other European powers sometimes squabbled with one another back in the Old World, such conflicts sometimes led to war. Usually these wars began in Europe and then spread secondarily to the warring nations' colonies in America.

The first three of these conflicts—King William's War, Queen Anne's War, and King George's War—set a pattern. The wars started in Europe; placed England and France against one another; and little of significance, especially in the New World, came of any of these three conflicts. However, by mid-eighteenth century another war erupted, the French and Indian War, and it was different, indeed. This time the war began in North America and spread to Europe. And, when it was all over, the European distribution of power in North America was forever changed.

THE LURE OF THE OHIO

For decades English colonials had hugged the Atlantic Coast, not venturing more than 50 to 100 miles (80 to 160 kilometers) inland. Their movement farther west was blocked by the long ridges of the Appalachian Mountains. However, by the 1740s, English colonials were looking beyond the mountain chain, setting their eyes on the Ohio Country, the region of the far frontier bounded by the Ohio River that flowed deep into the North American continent. Anyone wanting to control the Ohio region would have to control the Ohio River, which was formed by the joining of two other rivers, the Monongahela and the Allegheny.

In 1753, the French began to move decisively from Canada into the region, building a string of forts from the Ohio River north to the Great Lakes. The first was Fort Presque Isle, along the southern banks of Lake Erie. Next came Fort LeBoeuf to the south, then Fort Verango on the Allegheny in 1754.

Both the French and the English saw the Ohio Country as their own. French explorers had roamed into the Ohio Valley as early as the late 1600s. At the same time, English colonial charters had generally established northern and southern boundaries for their colonies, but no western boundary, so the English thought of their Atlantic colonies as extending into the Ohio Country and beyond.

WASHINGTON'S MISSION

In October 1753, to counter French "aggression" into the Ohio Country, Lieutenant Governor Robert Dinwiddie of Virginia dispatched a 21-year-old, untried colonial militia officer into the western wilderness to deliver an official letter that insisted the French remove themselves from the Ohio Country. The young colonel soon took his first walk on the stage of U.S. history: His name was George Washington, and he already had knowledge of the region from his time as a surveyor's apprentice.

Taking only a small party along, Washington marched into the heavily forested lands of western Virginia and Pennsylvania with his message from Dinwiddie. He reached Fort LeBoeuf, where he was politely received and then dismissed. The French were in the Ohio Country to stay and had, in fact, taken over a fort that a group of Virginians had been constructing at the headwaters of the important Ohio River.

Dinwiddie sent Washington back into the region the following spring, this time to march to the fort his fellow Virginians were constructing. (In the meantime, the French had taken it over and named it Fort Duquesne.) The young Virginian headed to the northwest escorted by 160 armed militiamen.

Along the way, Washington, now a lieutenant colonel, encountered a group of Mingo Indians under the leadership of a sachem named Tanaghrisson, or "Half King." Tanaghrisson hated the French, claiming that they had captured, boiled, and eaten his father. He informed Washington that the fort he was headed for was already in the hands of 1,000 French Canadians. He also told him that a party of Frenchmen was close by, numbering about 32 in all. Although he had orders not to act as the aggressor during his march into the wilderness, Washington decided to surprise attack the French group.

A FATEFUL DECISION

On May 28, 1754, Washington and his men met the French in an early morning attack. The French became aware of the Virginians' advance and, during a few tense moments, both sides had opened fire. It is not even clear which side fired the first shots. The fight went in Washington's favor, with 14 Frenchmen wounded or killed, and no Virginian casualties. Soon Washington was locked in surrender negotiations with the captured leader of the French party, Joseph Coulon, the Sieur de Jumonville (the young lieutenant colonel spoke no French). All had gone well so far, but suddenly Tanaghrisson turned on the French captives, his men ready to take their scalps. Before Washington could stop his Indian allies, Tanaghrisson killed the French leader with a war club. (The Half King's motivation is not certain. Perhaps he was trying to incite a larger scale conflict.) Washington's quick little wilderness battle had become a frontier massacre.

Tanaghrisson and his men abandoned Washington. According to historian James L. Roark, the Indian leader later stated of the young Virginian: "The Colonel was a good-natured man, but had no experience; he took upon him to command the Indians as his slaves, [and] would by no means take advice from the Indians." Washington had little choice but to continue his march, even though he feared the few French who had escaped the fight would soon tell their story and the French would march out to meet him with a superior force. About 60 miles (100 kilometers) short of Fort Duquesne, Washington and his men stopped to build a makeshift fort of their own. Reinforcements brought their numbers to more than 300 men.

UNDER ATTACK

On July 3 the French attacked. The French and their Indian allies found Washington's men unprepared, with many sick and hungry. The fort was not finished and had been built in a poor, low-lying location. Recent rains had left much of the Virginians' powder wet. Thirty of Washington's men were killed and another 70 were wounded. The young militia officer surrendered to the French the following day, July 4. When Washington signed the surrender documents, which were in French, he did not know that he was admitting to wantonly killing a French ambassador, namely Jumonville. As the papers made their way from Canada to Paris and to other European capitals, the name "George Washington" was soon seen as one of treachery and murder. Washington was not famous, but infamous.

In reality, Jumonville was not a professional diplomat. He had actually been sent into the Pennsylvania wilderness with a message to the Virginia governor, just as Washington had carried a message from the Virginia lieutenant governor the previous year. Yet the story was told, and the French reacted directly to the wilderness attack on one of their own on western soil they also considered their own. Events accelerated, and Great Britain and France fell into war with one another.

THE ALBANY PLAN OF UNION

As the threat of war loomed again in the colonies, some colonial leaders—including representatives from New York, Pennsylvania, Maryland, and the New England colonies—met together in Albany, New York, to discuss possible strategies. Those present included Benjamin Franklin from Philadelphia and Thomas Hutchinson from Massachusetts. They set a priority on convincing the Iroquois Indians to band with them against the French in case of war.

George Washington as a colonel in the Virginia militia, painted in 1772 by artist, soldier, and naturalist Charles Willson Peale (1741–1827). Peale produced more than 50 portraits of Washington.

Franklin, by then one of the most well-known men in the colonies due to his work as a printer and publisher of a popular almanac, suggested also that the colonies form the Albany Plan of Union. This would create an intercolonial council that could have the power to tax the colonies as members. However, the plan was not accepted by the majority of colonial leaders. Most colonies were not prepared to surrender some of their power to a confederacy of colonies. They also failed to convince the Iroquois to join with them, convincing only one of the six nations of the Iroquois, the Mohawk, to their side.

BRADDOCK'S MARCH

The war arrived in 1755, and Great Britain dispatched thousands of troops to the colonies. They arrived under the command of General Edward Braddock, a veteran of European fighting, who had served since the latter days of the War of the Spanish Succession. The 60-year-old Braddock was determined to march into the same wilderness where Washington had already fought and lost, heading his men toward Fort Duquesne. By June, his 1,400 red-coated, British regular troops were on their way, along with 450 Virginia militiamen, led by George Washington.

With so many men on the move, Braddock could hardly expect to surprise the French. Taking along supply wagons and heavy cannon, he ordered Redcoat axe men to fell trees ahead of the main column, in effect building a road of sorts as they marched. With all that noise, the French knew well in advance where Braddock was. They did not remain in Fort Duquesne, which was a simple, crude fort of logs and clapboard. The French knew they would have to face Braddock in the field. It would be a field of their choosing.

By early July, Braddock and his men were only eight miles (13 kilometers) from Fort Duquesne, and it was here that the French and their Indian allies attacked. They caught the British and the Virginians making their way along a winding, snakelike Indian trail, with troops lined up almost in a single column. In their surprise attack, 650 Indians and several dozen Frenchmen opened fire. The British could not form up as they normally would have during a European battle, and panic spread quickly among the men. With the Indians firing from behind trees and rocks, the British could not even see their foes.

Braddock tried to keep his men in the open, ordering them to line up and fire in volleys, or in unison. This made the British constant targets. In the confusion, some British troops even fired on one another. Braddock was shot during the fight. George Washington, however, managed to keep his cool and organize the retreat. Although personally unharmed, the young militia officer had two horses shot out from under him, and bullets ripped through his coat on four occasions. Before the fight was over, the British left behind nearly 900 of their men, either dead or wounded, many of whom were scalped. Braddock died three days after the battle and was buried on the trail. His men ran wagons over the gravesite, so that Indians would not discover it and mutilate the corpse. The first large-scale battle of the French and Indian War had ended in utter defeat for the British and their colonial subjects.

THE WAR IN AMERICA

Braddock had been defeated by his own lack of imagination. He did not listen to Washington's advice that he might need to fight differently in America. It was a mistake that cost him his life. Over the next few years the war continued as badly for the British as it had begun. The French and their Indian allies repeatedly attacked English colonial settlements across the frontier. They also built more forts, including Fort Saint

Frédéric on Lake Champlain, with its stout stone walls and four-story bombproof tower, the entire facility bristling with 40 cannon. On Lake George's north banks, they occupied Fort Carillon (later known to the British as Fort Ticonderoga). Such sites provided garrison posts for thousands of white-uniformed French troops.

The British authorities dispatched Lord Loudoun (his name was John Campbell) to the colonies to lead the fight, while the French sent one of their greatest heroes of war, General Louis Montcalm. He had participated in so many

Siege and Massacre at Fort William Henry

The British built Fort William Henry on the southern banks of Lake George during the winter of 1756–57. It was constructed of pine logs inside and out, with earth filling the spaces between, creating walls that measured 30 feet (9 meters) thick. A 30-foot-wide (9-m) ditch surrounded the fort. Located strategically, William Henry soon became a thorn in the side of the French. It had to be taken.

General Montcalm marched from Fort Carillon to William Henry with more than 2,500 regular French troops, almost 2,500 French Canadian militia, 300 volunteers, and at least 1,500 Indian allies. The French also brought along 36 cannon and four mortars. Defending the fort,

under the command of Lieutenant Colonel George Monro, were nearly 2,400 men. As the fort was only large enough to hold 500, most were situated outside the walls in makeshift trench works.

By early August, the siege was on. The English sent to neighboring Fort Edward for reinforcements, but its commander, General Daniel Webb, locked himself inside his fort and never lifted a finger to help.

Between August 3 and 7, the French poured artillery fire against Fort William Henry and dug zigzagging trenches that inched them closer and closer to the fort's walls, allowing the mortars to blow the fort apart. By August 8, the French battles in Europe that his body was littered with scars. In New York, Montcalm led French troops against British forts, including Fort Oswego on Lake Ontario, which they burned in 1756 and, the following year, Fort William Henry, on Lake George. Here, the French laid siege to the British post until it fell into their hands. (The U.S. author James Fenimore Cooper used the siege as a backdrop for his 1826 novel, *The Last of the Mohicans*.) Following the fall of Fort William Henry, the French marched just 10 miles (16 kilometers) away and captured Fort Edward.

had dug their trench lines to within 250 yards (230 meters) of the fort. The British were running out of ammunition, and morale was low. Monro finally surrendered to the French on August 9.

Montcalm gave generous terms to the defenders of Fort William Henry. They were allowed to leave as long as they promised not to fight for the next 18 months, and promised a French escort to Fort Edward. But as the British troops, colonial militiamen, and civilians left the fort, they were attacked by Indian allies of the French. Angry that Montcalm's terms did not allow them to take any spoils of war, the Indians stripped the defeated British of anything they could, including clothes, weapons, ammunition, supplies, food, and alcohol. As one Massachusetts militiaman described the attack, as noted by historian Walter Borneman, "The savages fell upon the rear, killing and scalping."

Just how many British were killed remains a controversy. Some eyewitness claims put the number as high as 1,500, but recent analysis suggests the number murdered was fewer than 200 and perhaps as low as 69. But the Indian attack, with victims including civilians who had taken refuge behind the fort's walls, cast a pall on the surrender of Fort William Henry. However, some of the British troops who were scalped had smallpox, which the Indians carried back to their homes, probably infecting and killing tens of thousands of American Indians.

THE BRITISH CHANGE TACK

For the first two or three years of the French and Indian War, the French advance was relentless. They gained control of not only the Ohio River Valley, but of much of northern New York. The war went so badly for the British that a new prime minister was brought to power in 1757—William Pitt, known to the British people as the "Great Commoner." Pitt immediately dispatched many more regular British forces, a troop surge that would ultimately pay off. He also sent greater quantities of supplies and war materiel. His aim was not only the acquisition of the Ohio Country, but of all of French Canada. He soon sent his most capable military commanders to the American front, including Major General Jeffrey Amherst.

By the summer of 1758 Amherst was on the move, capturing Fort Louisbourg, which guarded the mouth of the St. Lawrence River. By summer's end he had captured Fort Frontenac on Lake Ontario, so the British had gained control of both ends of the St. Lawrence. Amherst then sent General John Forbes with four companies of Royal Americans, 2,000 provincial troops, 1,000 Highland Scots, and 500 Cherokee warriors to capture Fort Duquesne at the headwaters of the Ohio River. As they approached, the French burned the fort. The British occupied the key ground anyway and soon built their own fort, naming it Fort Pitt in honor of the prime minister. (The site would one day become the city of Pittsburgh.)

THE TURNING TIDE

By 1759 the French were on the defensive. They had lost control of the Ohio River Valley and, out in the far west, the Mississippi River. English armies captured Fort Niagara, Fort Saint Frédéric (which they renamed Crown Point), and Fort Carillon (renamed Ticonderoga) with sheer numbers of men. The Fort Carillon campaign alone required 12,000 British forces.

The actions of General Amherst became legendary. Typically, he took no quarter with captured Indians who had allied themselves with the French, ordering their executions. He justified his extremes as retaliation for the massacre of British troops and colonials at the hands of Indians following the surrender of Fort William Henry.

By 1759 the majority of French forts were in British hands and only two key French bastions were left—the cities of Montreal and Quebec, both situated along the St. Lawrence River. General Amherst understood the significance of these two French holdouts, writing a letter to William Pitt in 1759, as noted by historian Walter Borneman, "by whatsoever avenue we succeed, Quebec or Montreal, Canada must fall, and with it everything on this side of the River St. Lawrence." But the campaigns against those two sites were given to another British general, 32-year-old James Wolfe, who had distinguished himself during the Louisbourg campaign. Wolfe was a younger man, of striking character with flaming red hair, and a skilled fighter.

ATTACK ON QUEBEC

Wolfe's first target was Quebec. Having served as a fur trading post during the 1600s, the city was situated atop high, steep cliffs that loomed above the St. Lawrence. The site was considered impossible to approach militarily. In addition, French General Montcalm had stationed his men there—a force that included 14,000 French regulars, marines, Canadian militia, and a small number of Indians. Wolfe had gathered forces numbering close to 12,000, including some of the best and fittest British troops then in North America.

Wolfe began moving his troops against Quebec during the summer of 1759. By the end of June, he had placed artillery batteries on islands in the St. Lawrence opposite the French town. A bombardment was begun, and several Quebec buildings were leveled. Then, Wolfe dispatched British Admiral Sir Charles Saunders to deliver several of his ships, including a pair of 40-gun frigates, upriver and past Quebec, to provide Wolfe with ultimate control of the river.

From his new position, Wolfe was able to get a close look at the bluff walls facing his men on the opposite bank of the St. Lawrence. He studied the rock faces, sometimes dressing as a regular enlisted soldier, so as not to draw attention from the French observation post at the top of the cliffs. Eventually, he spotted a narrow, natural path running from the heights to the river front. He convinced himself that several units of Scottish Highlanders could be ferried across the St. Lawrence at night, then scale the 180-foot-tall (55-meter) cliffs using this precarious rocky staircase. It was September, and Wolfe knew his men must be sent forward soon or the river would freeze over, leaving him and his men stranded on the wrong side of the river. He set the date for his attack for September 13, 1759.

THE PLAINS OF ABRAHAM

In the early morning hours, Wolfe's men began moving toward the cliffs. By 6 A.M. nearly 5,000 troops had scaled the cliff side and assembled themselves on the level ground south of Quebec, a stretch of land known as the Plains of Abraham. (The name was not taken from the Old Testament patriarch, but to honor one of the French explorer Champlain's river pilots, Abraham Martin.) By the time Montcalm realized the British troops had reached the heights, he felt he had little choice but to come out of the city, which was located two miles (three kilometers) away, and engage the enemy. (Montcalm could have chosen to remain in the city, for Quebec was in an excellent position to withstand a siege laid down by Wolfe's men. Winter probably would have arrived before the surrender of the city, which would have made things extremely difficult for the British.)

The battle was typical for two European armies. They approached one another in well-ordered, straight columns of men, the British dressed in red and the French in white. Wolfe ordered his men to charge forward, and Montcalm's troops responded with a musket volley that was premature, allowing the British to continue their advance until they were within 20 yards (18 meters) of their enemy. Only then

At the Battle of Quebec, British forces scaled the cliffs and formed up on the Plains of Abraham. Major General Wolfe commanded around 4,500 men and one gun. The Marquis de Montcalm brought to the battle a force of around 5,000 men and three guns.

did they open with a withering fire. The French line immediately wavered, then fell apart, the soldiers retreating from
the field of battle.

Both Wolfe and Montcalm received mortal wounds during the fight. Montcalm was wounded in his abdomen and
his leg, which was ripped apart by grapeshot, while Wolfe
received wounds to the chest and intestines during a bay-
onet charge. Wolfe died on the battlefield that day, while
Montcalm remained alive until the next morning. Before
their deaths, they each left words to be remembered. Wolfe
noted he could die happy since he had won the battle, and

THE COST OF WAR

As the British emerged victorious
and having gained a vast empire
in the New World, storm clouds
were gathering. Officials began
counting the costs of the prolonged
conflict, which had involved tens
of thousands of British troops and
colonials, hundreds of ships, and
millions of pounds of equipment,
arms, and supplies—and the sum
was staggering. Prior to the war,
the English national debt had stood
near 73 million pounds. By the war's
end, that had nearly doubled to 137
million pounds (an amount close to
20 billion dollars today). The British
had won a strategic war, but at what
cost? How could such a debt be paid?

People in Great Britain could
hardly afford to pay any more in
taxes. By 1760, residents of the
British Isles were already paying
30 times more in taxes than their
English counterparts in America.
The British Crown wasted little time
coming to an obvious conclusion:
The war had been fought, in part,
to protect the colonies from French
encroachment so the colonies would
have to begin paying their fair share
to help cover the debts accumulated
through that war. The conflict that
would emerge between Great Britain
and its uncooperative colonial
subjects would ultimately lead to the
American Revolution.

Montcalm expressed relief he would not live to see Quebec in the hands of the British.

In the course of the battle of Quebec, about 60 British soldiers were killed and 600 wounded. Two hundred Frenchmen were killed, along with 1,200 wounded.

THE END OF THE WAR

Four days after the battle, the French officially surrendered Quebec to the British. It was clear the loss of the city signaled the outcome of the French and Indian War. The following year the British captured Montreal, the last significant French stronghold in Canada. But the war's end did not come for another two years. Most of the later fighting was centered in Europe, where the conflict would be called the Seven Years War. It all might have ended earlier if a new British monarch had had his way. In 1760, George II died and left the throne to his grandson, George III. The young king considered calling for an immediate end to the hostilities, but Prime Minister Pitt managed to talk him out of it. Pitt was ultimately replaced, but the war continued until 1763.

When a peace treaty was finally signed in Paris, the British emerged the clear winner. The French were forced to cede, or grant ownership, of all of Canada to the British, effectively ending a century of French power over Canada. In addition, France's main ally, Spain, was required to surrender Florida to Britain. The British also mandated that the French cede the great western region of Louisiana, lands that stretched from the Mississippi River to the Rocky Mountains of the Far West, to the Spanish. At the time, the British were in no position to take control of Louisiana, but they were intent on wresting the region out from under French dominance. The French and Indian War, along with its European counterpart, the Seven Years War, had ended with a great victory for the British and a huge power shift in North America.

Chronology

1492 Christopher Columbus reaches the Western Hemisphere

1497 John Cabot sails to modern-day Canada on behalf of England

1523–24 French King Francis I sponsors explorer Giovanni da Verrazano to sail to North America in search of the Northwest Passage

TIMELINE

1492
Christopher Columbus reaches the Western Hemisphere

1565
Spanish establish outpost at St. Augustine in Florida

1607
Founding of English colonies at Jamestown

1608
Establishment of French colony of Quebec

| 1492 | 1525 | 1550 | 1575 | 1600 | 1625 |

1497
John Cabot sails to modern-day Canada on behalf of England

1534–42
Jacques Cartier explores eastern Canada for France

1587
Founding of "Lost Colony" of Roanoke

1620
The Pilgrims found the Plymouth colony in New England

1534–42 Jacques Cartier explores eastern Canada for France

1562 French naval officer, Jean Ribault, establishes colony along Florida's St. John's River

1565 Spanish establish outpost at St. Augustine in Florida

1587 Founding of "Lost Colony" of Roanoke

1588 English defeat of the Spanish Armada

1598 Spanish found colony in New Mexico

1603–08 French explorer Champlain founds settlement in Canada

1607 Founding of English colonies at Jamestown and Sagadahoc

1634
Cecilius Calvert founds his proprietary colony of Maryland

1635–36
Roger Williams founds Providence, Rhode Island

1636
First English settlements in Connecticut

1692–93
Salem witchcraft trials

1702
Delaware becomes a separate colony

1759
Quebec falls to British forces

1755–63
French and Indian War in America

| 1626 | 1650 | 1675 | 1700 | 1725 | 1763 |

1663
The colony of Carolina is established

1681
Pennsylvania colony is established

1732
Georgia colony is established

1664
New Netherland is taken by the English and converted into New York. Colony of New Jersey is also established

Chronology

1608 Establishment of French colony of Quebec in modern-day Canada

1609–10 Captain Henry Hudson explores eastern Canada and modern-day New York

1614 Captain John Smith names New England

1619 Arrival of first Africans at Jamestown. The Virginia House of Burgesses is established

1620 The Pilgrims found the Plymouth colony in New England. The *Mayflower* Compact is signed

1624 The Dutch establish the colony of New Netherland

1625 Fort Amsterdam is founded

1630 The Massachusetts Bay Colony is founded

1630–42 The Great Migration to New England

1634 Cecilius Calvert founds his proprietary colony of Maryland

1635–36 Roger Williams, banished from the Massachusetts Bay Colony, founds Providence, Rhode Island

1636 First English settlements in Connecticut

1637 The Pequot War is fought in New England

1638 New Haven colony is founded

1649 Maryland's Act for Religious Toleration is passed

1660s Settlements are established in North Carolina

1662 "Halfway Covenant" is adopted by Massachusetts clergy

1663 The colony of Carolina is established

1664 New Netherland is taken by the English and converted into New York. Colony of New Jersey is also established

1670s Settlements are established in South Carolina. East and West Jersey become separate colonies

1673 French explorers reach the Mississippi River from Canada

1675–76 King Philip's War in New England is fought

1676 Bacon's Rebellion takes place in Virginia

1681 Pennsylvania colony is established

1689 English Parliament passes the Toleration Act

1689–97 King William's War in America

1692–93 Salem witchcraft trials take place in
Massachusetts

1701 The Jerseys are reunited as a royal colony

1702 Delaware becomes a separate colony

1702–13 Queen Anne's War in America

1718 New Orleans founded

1732 Georgia colony is established

1730s–1740s The Great Awakening takes place in America

1744–48 King George's War in America

1754 George Washington is defeated at Fort Necessity.
Albany Conference takes place in New York

1755 General Braddock is defeated near Fort Duquesne

1755–63 French and Indian War in America

1757 Siege of Fort William Henry takes place. William Pitt
becomes new prime minister of Great Britain

1759 Quebec falls to British forces

1760 Montreal falls to the British

Glossary

aristocracy The upper class of a society into which one is born; a rank providing lifelong privilege.

Cathay An alternative European name for China.

colonization The process of one nation taking control of a foreign state and its peoples by establishing its own settlements, or colonies.

confederation A group of tribes, colonies, or states working together for the common good.

Congregationalists A later name for "Puritans."

covenant A solemn agreement or promise.

freemen Men who were not bound to another and had the right to vote.

frontier The uncivilized, unchartered region beyond the settled lands.

Great Awakening Religious movement of the 1730s and 40s, centered in England and the thirteen colonies, which emphasized greater Christian commitment and a greater personal spiritual and emotional relationship with God.

Halfway Covenant Plan adopted in 1662 by New England clergy to deal with declining church membership, allowing an adult to be baptized if his or her parents were church members, even without a conversion experience.

headright system A system of land distribution which granted land to anyone who paid his or her passage to America.

hiving out Process by which the New England colonists spread out, establishing new towns and settlements.

Huguenots French Protestants.

indentured servants Generally poor English immigrants to America who, not being able to afford to pay their own ship passage, instead offered their labor as a servant to pay for the journey. Most served seven years, then received their freedom.

indigenous Native; originally from that land.

joint-stock company A business venture financed by the sale of stock by investors. The establishment of some New World colonies was financed this way.

margrave A European title or rank, referring to a military governor.

natural increase When a population group increases in number because its birth rate is higher than its death rate.

patent An official title of land, usually granted by a monarch.

Pilgrims A term referring to the Puritans or, more accurately, Separatists who immigrated to America in 1620 onboard the *Mayflower*.

proprietary colony A colony under the leadership and control of a designated individual proprietor or group of proprietors.

Protestants Religious groups that emerged out of the Reformation movement in Europe during the sixteenth and seventeenth centuries. They protested at many beliefs and customs of the Roman Catholic Church.

Puritans Members of the Church of England who believed the church needed to be simplified, or purified. Facing persecution at home, a sect of this religious group—the Separatists—settled in New England.

Glossary

Reformation A religious movement in Europe which began in the 1500s as a protest of the practices and theologies of the Roman Catholic Church.

royal charter Permission granted by a monarch to establish a colony.

scurvy A disease caused by a deficiency of vitamin C.

Separatists A term sometimes used to refer to Puritans who separated from the Church of England, rather than continuing to try to purify its practices.

theology A religious concept or belief.

toleration Acceptance of other beliefs, for example religious ideals.

Bibliography

Bonomi, Patricia U. *Under the Cope of Heaven: Religion, Society, and Politics in Colonial America.* New York: Oxford University Press, 1986.

Borneman, Walter R. *The French and Indian War: Deciding the Fate of North America.* New York: HarperCollins Publishers, 2006.

Carpenter, Edmund Jones. *The Mayflower Pilgrims.* New York: The Abingdon Press, 1918.

Costain, Thomas B. *The White and the Gold: The French Regime in Canada.* Garden City, NY: Doubleday & Company, 1954.

Crawford, Mary Caroline. *In the Days of the Pilgrim Fathers.* Boston: Little, Brown, and Company, 1921.

Cumming, W. P. *The Discovery of North America.* New York: American Heritage Press, 1972.

Flexner, Thomas. *Washington: The Indispensable Man.* Boston: Little, Brown and Company, 1974.

Gipson, Lawrence Henry. *The British Empire Before the American Revolution*, Volume 7, *The Victorious Years, 1758–1760.* New York: Knopf, 1949.

Heilbroner, Robert and Aaron Singer. *The Economic Transformation of America, 1600 to the Present.* Fort Worth: Harcourt Brace College Publishers, 1994.

Hoffer, Peter Charles. *The Brave New World: A History of Early America.* Boston: Houghton Mifflin Company, 2000.

Horn, James. *A Land as God Made It: Jamestown and the Birth of America.* New York: Basic Books, 2005.

Kluger, Richard. *Seizing Destiny: How America Grew from Sea to Shining Sea.* New York: Alfred A. Knopf, 2007.

Laudonnière, René Goulaine de. *A Foothold in Florida: The Eye-Witness Account of Four Voyages Made by the French* to That Region and Their Attempt at Colonisation, 1562–1568, based on L'Histoire Notable de la Floride. West Sussex, UK: Antique Atlas Publications, 1992.

McNeese, Tim. *Jamestown.* New York: Chelsea House Publishers, 2007.

———. *Plymouth.* New York: Chelsea House Publishers, 2007.

———. *The St. Lawrence River.* Philadelphia: Chelsea House Publishers, 2005.

Milton, Giles. *Big Chief Elizabeth: The Adventures and Fate of the First English Colonists in America.* New York: Farrar, Straus and Giroux, 2000.

Morison, Samuel Eliot. *Builders of the Bay Colony.* Boston: Houghton Mifflin Company, 1958.

———. *The European Discovery of America: The Southern Voyages, A.D. 1492–1616.* New York: Oxford University Press, 1993.

Philbrick, Nathaniel. *Mayflower: A Story of Courage, Community, and War.* New York: Viking Group, 2006.

Rhodes, Neil, et al. *King James VI and I: Selected Writings.* Farnham, UK: Ashgate Publishing, 2004.

Roark, James L. et al. *The American Promise: A History of the United States.* Volume I. Boston: Bedford/St. Martin's, 2009.

Shorto, Russell. *The Island at the Center of the World: The Epic Story of Dutch Manhattan and the Forgotten Colony That Shaped America.* New York: Random House, Inc., 2004.

Smith, John. *A Description of New England.* In *Captain John Smith: Writings: with Selected narratives of the Exploration and Settlement of Virginia,* Library of America series. New York: Penguin Group (USA), 2007.

———. *Generall Historie of Virginia.* In *Captain John Smith: Writings: with Selected narratives of the Exploration and Settlement of Virginia,* Library of America series. New York: Penguin Group (USA), 2007.

———. *Travels and Works of Captain John Smith, Volume I: President of Virginia, and Admiral of New England 1580–*

1631. Edward Arber, Ed. Whitefish, MT: Kessinger Publishing Company, 2007.

Stout, Harry S. *The New England Soul: Preaching and Religious Culture in Colonial New England.* New York: Oxford University Press, 1988.

Usher, Roland G. *The Pilgrims and Their History.* Williamstown, MA: Corner House Publishers, 1977.

Weinstein, Allen. *The Story of America: Freedom and Crisis From Settlement to Superpower.* New York: DK Publishing, Inc., 2002.

Wrong, George M. *The Rise and Fall of New France,* Vol. 1. New York: Octagon Books, 1970.

Further Resources

Alderman, Clifford Lindsey. *The Story of the Thirteen Colonies.*
New York: Random House, 1966.

Baczynski, Bernadette L. *William Penn.* Mankato, MN:
Coughlan Publishing, 2000.

Fritz, Jean. *The Lost Colony of Roanoke.* New York:
Penguin Group (USA), 2004.

Hakim, Joy. *History of U.S.: Making Thirteen Colonies.*
New York: Oxford University Press, 2007.

Hillstrom, Laurie Collier. *French and Indian War.*
San Diego: Gale Group, 2003.

Jehle, Paul. *Plymouth in the Words of Her Founders.*
San Antonio: The Vision Forum, 2003.

Laager, Hollie. *The French and Indian War.* Vero Beach,
FL: Rourke Publishing, LLC., 2006.

McNeese, Tim. *George Washington: America's Leader in War
and Peace.* New York: Chelsea House Publishers, 2006.

———. *New Amsterdam.* New York: Chelsea House
Publishers, 2007.

———. *Williamsburg.* New York: Chelsea House
Publishers, 2007.

Mello, Tara Baukus. *John Smith.* Philadelphia:
Chelsea House Publishers, 2000.

Molzahn, Arlene Bourgeois. *Henry Hudson: Explorer of
the Hudson River.* Berkeley Heights, NJ:
Enslow Publishers, Inc., 2003.

Nobleman, Marc Tyler. *Thirteen Colonies.*
Mankato, MN: Coughlan Publishing, 2002.

North, Sterling. *George Washington: Frontier Colonel.*
New York: Sterling Publishing, 2006.

Petrie, Kristin. *Henry Hudson.* Edina, MN:
ABDO Publishing, 2007.

Stratton, Eugene Aubrey. *Plymouth Colony: Its History and People*. Ancestry.com, 1997.

Worland, Gayle. *Let Freedom Ring!: The Jamestown Colony*. Mankato, MN: Capstone Press, 2004.

Web sites

History Globe—Jamestown:
http://www.historyglobe.com/jamestown/

Holidays on the Net—Thanksgiving:
http://www.holidays.net/thanksgiving/pilgrims.html

Jamestown Rediscovery:
http://www.apva.org/jr.html

Jamestown–Yorktown Foundation:
http://historyisfun.org/Jamestown-Settlement.htm

Mayflower Families:
http://www.mayflowerfamilies.com/

Mayflower History:
http://www.mayflowerhistory.com/History/history.php

Native Americans—Wampanoag:
http://www.nativeamericans.com/Wampanoag.htm

Plimoth Plantation:
http://www.plimoth.org/

Virginia's James River Plantations:
http://www.jamesriverplantations.org/

Virtual Jamestown:
http://www.virtualjamestown.org/

Williamsburg:
http://www.williamsburg.com

Picture Credits

Index

About the Author

Tim McNeese is associate professor of history at York College in York, Nebraska. Professor McNeese holds degrees from York College, Harding University, and Missouri State University. He has published more than 100 books and educational materials. His writing has earned him a citation in the library reference work, *Contemporary Authors* and multiple citations in *Best Books for Young Teen Readers*. In 2006, Tim appeared on the History Channel program, *Risk Takers, History Makers: John Wesley Powell and the Grand Canyon*. He was been a faculty member at the Tony Hillerman Writers Conference in Albuquerque. His wife, Beverly, is assistant professor of English at York College. They have two married children, Noah and Summer, and three grandchildren—Ethan, Adrianna, and Finn William. Tim and Bev have sponsored college study trips on the Lewis and Clark Trail and to the American Southwest. You may contact Professor McNeese at tdmcneese@york.edu.

About the Consultant

Richard Jensen is Research Professor at Montana State University, Billings. He has published 11 books on a wide range of topics in American political, social, military, and economic history, as well as computer methods. After taking a Ph.D. at Yale in 1966, he taught at numerous universities, including Washington, Michigan, Harvard, Illinois-Chicago, West Point, and Moscow State University in Russia.